Table of Contents

Appendices

List of Tables and Figures

The World Wide Web (WWW) is a system for exchanging information over the Internet. At the most basic level, the Web can be divided into two principal components: Web servers, which are applications that make information available over the Internet (in essence, publish information), and Web browsers (clients), which are used to access and display the information stored on the Web servers. This document focuses on the security issues of Web servers.[1]

Unfortunately, Web servers are often the most targeted and attacked hosts on organizations' networks. As a result, it is essential to secure Web servers and the network infrastructure that supports them. The following are examples of specific security threats to Web servers:

- Malicious entities may exploit software bugs in the Web server, underlying operating system, or active content to gain unauthorized access to the Web server. Examples of this unauthorized access include gaining access to files or folders that were not meant to be publicly accessible (e.g., directory traversal attacks) and being able to execute commands and/or install software on the Web server.

- Denial of service (DoS) attacks may be directed to the Web server or its supporting network infrastructure, denying or hindering valid users from making use of its services.

- Sensitive information on the Web server may be read or modified without authorization.

- Sensitive information on backend databases that are used to support interactive elements of a Web application may be compromised through command injection attacks (e.g., Structured Query Language [SQL] injection, Lightweight Directory Access Protocol (LDAP) injection, cross-site scripting [XSS]).

- Sensitive information transmitted unencrypted between the Web server and the browser may be intercepted.

- Information on the Web server may be changed for malicious purposes. Web site defacement is a commonly reported example of this threat.

- Malicious entities may gain unauthorized access to resources elsewhere in the organization's network via a successful attack on the Web server.

- Malicious entities may attack external entities after compromising a Web server host. These attacks can be launched directly (e.g., from the compromised host against an external server) or indirectly (e.g., placing malicious content on the compromised Web server that attempts to exploit vulnerabilities in the Web browsers of users visiting the site).

- The server may be used as a distribution point for attack tools, pornography, or illegally copied software.

Web servers may also face indirect attacks to gain information from their users. In these attacks, the user is persuaded or automatically directed to visit a malicious Web site that appears to be legitimate. The identifying information that is harvested may be used to access the Web site itself or form the basis for

---

[1] For more information on securing Web browsers, see NIST Special Publication 800-46, *Security for Telecommuting and Broadband Communications* (http://csrc.nist.gov/publications/nistpubs/).

identity theft. Successful attacks can compromise confidential Web site resources or harm an organization's image. These indirect attacks occur in two forms:

■ Phishing, where attackers use social engineering to trick users into logging into a fake site

■ Pharming, where Domain Name System (DNS) servers or users' host files are compromised to redirect users to a malicious site in place of the legitimate site.

This document is intended to assist organizations in installing, configuring, and maintaining secure public Web servers. More specifically, this document describes, in detail, the following practices to apply:

■ Securing, installing, and configuring the underlying operating system

■ Securing, installing, and configuring Web server software

■ Deploying appropriate network protection mechanisms, such as firewalls, routers, switches, and intrusion detection and intrusion prevention systems

■ Maintaining the secure configuration through application of appropriate patches and upgrades, security testing, monitoring of logs, and backups of data and operating system files

■ Using, publicizing, and protecting information and data in a careful and systematic manner.

The following key guidelines are recommended to Federal departments and agencies for maintaining a secure Web presence.

Organizations should carefully plan and address the security aspects of the deployment of a public Web server.

Because it is much more difficult to address security once deployment and implementation have occurred, security should be considered from the initial planning stage. Organizations are more likely to make decisions about configuring computers appropriately and consistently when they develop and use a detailed, well-designed deployment plan. Developing such a plan will support Web server administrators in making the inevitable tradeoff decisions between usability, performance, and risk.

Organizations often fail to consider the human resource requirements for both deployment and operational phases of the Web server and supporting infrastructure. Organizations should address the following points in a deployment plan:

■ Types of personnel required (e.g., system and Web server administrators, Webmasters, network administrators, information systems security officers [ISSO])

■ Skills and training required by assigned personnel

■ Individual (i.e., level of effort required of specific personnel types) and collective staffing (i.e., overall level of effort) requirements.

Organizations should implement appropriate security management practices and controls when maintaining and operating a secure Web server.

Appropriate management practices are essential to operating and maintaining a secure Web server. Security practices entail the identification of an organization's information system assets and the development, documentation, and implementation of policies, standards, procedures, and guidelines that help to ensure the confidentiality, integrity, and availability of information system resources. To ensure the security of a Web server and the supporting network infrastructure, the following practices should be implemented:

■ Organization-wide information system security policy

■ Configuration/change control and management

■ Risk assessment and management

■ Standardized software configurations that satisfy the information system security policy

■ Security awareness and training

■ Contingency planning, continuity of operations, and disaster recovery planning

■ Certification and accreditation.

Organizations should ensure that Web server operating systems are deployed, configured, and managed to meet the security requirements of the organization.

The first step in securing a Web server is securing the underlying operating system. Most commonly available Web servers operate on a general-purpose operating system. Many security issues can be avoided if the operating systems underlying Web servers are configured appropriately. Default hardware and software configurations are typically set by manufacturers to emphasize features, functions, and ease of use, at the expense of security. Because manufacturers are not aware of each organization's security needs, each Web server administrator must configure new servers to reflect their organization's security requirements and reconfigure them as those requirements change. Using security configuration guides or checklists can assist administrators in securing systems consistently and efficiently. Securing an operating system initially would generally include the following steps:

■ Patch and upgrade the operating system

■ Remove or disable unnecessary services and applications

■ Configure operating system user authentication

■ Configure resource controls

■ Install and configure additional security controls

■ Perform security testing of the operating system.

Organizations should ensure that the Web server application is deployed, configured, and managed to meet the security requirements of the organization.

In many respects, the secure installation and configuration of the Web server application will mirror the operating system process discussed above. The overarching principle is to install the minimal amount of Web server services required and eliminate any known vulnerabilities through patches or upgrades. If the installation program installs any unnecessary applications, services, or scripts, they should be removed immediately after the installation process concludes. Securing the Web server application would generally include the following steps:

- Patch and upgrade the Web server application

- Remove or disable unnecessary services, applications, and sample content

- Configure Web server user authentication and access controls

- Configure Web server resource controls

- Test the security of the Web server application and Web content.

Organizations should take steps to ensure that only appropriate content is published on a Web site.

Many agencies lack a Web publishing process or policy that determines what type of information to publish openly, what information to publish with restricted access, and what information should not be published to any publicly accessible repository. This is unfortunate because Web sites are often one of the first places that malicious entities search for valuable information. Some generally accepted examples of what should not be published or at least should be carefully examined and reviewed before publication on a public Web site include—

- Classified or proprietary information

- Information on the composition or preparation of hazardous materials or toxins[2]

- Sensitive information relating to homeland security

- Medical records

- An organization's detailed physical and information security safeguards

- Details about an organization's network and information system infrastructure (e.g., address ranges, naming conventions, access numbers)

- Information that specifies or implies physical security vulnerabilities

- Detailed plans, maps, diagrams, aerial photographs, and architectural drawings of organizational buildings, properties, or installations

- Any sensitive information about individuals, such as personally identifiable information (PII), that might be subject to either Federal, state or, in some instances, international privacy laws.[3]

Organizations should ensure appropriate steps are taken to protect Web content from unauthorized access or modification.

---

[2] For more guidance on protecting this type of information, see the White House Memorandum dated March 19, 2000, *Action to Safeguard Information Regarding Weapons of Mass Destruction and Other Sensitive Documents Related to Homeland Security* (http://www.usdoj.gov/oip/foiapost/2002foiapost10.htm).

[3] For more guidance on protecting this type of information, see OMB Memorandum M-06-16 and OMB Memorandum M-07-16 at http://www.whitehouse.gov/omb/memoranda/.

Although information on public Web sites is content that is intended to be public, assuming a credible review process and policy is in place, it is still important to ensure that information cannot be modified without authorization. Users of this information rely upon the integrity of such information even if the information is not confidential. Because of the public accessibility, content on publicly accessible Web servers is inherently more vulnerable than information that is inaccessible from the Internet. This vulnerability means that organizations need to protect public Web content through the appropriate configuration of Web server resource controls. Examples of resource control practices include—

- Install or enable only necessary services.

- Install Web content on a dedicated hard drive or logical partition.

- Limit uploads to directories that are not readable by the Web server.

- Define a single directory for all external scripts or programs executed as part of Web content.

- Disable the use of hard or symbolic links.

- Define a complete Web content access matrix that identifies which folders and files within the Web server document directory are restricted and which are accessible (and by whom).

- Disable directory listings.

- Use user authentication, digital signatures, and other cryptographic mechanisms as appropriate.

- Use host-based intrusion detection systems (IDS), intrusion prevention systems (IPS), and/or file integrity checkers to detect intrusions and verify Web content.

- Protect each backend server (e.g., database server, directory server) from command injection attacks at both the Web server and the backend server.

Organizations should use active content judiciously after balancing the benefits gained against the associated risks.

Most early Web sites presented static information residing on the server, typically in the form of text-based documents. Soon thereafter, interactive elements were introduced to offer users new ways to interact with a Web site. Unfortunately, these same interactive elements introduced new Web-related vulnerabilities because they involve dynamically executing code on either the Web server or client using a large number of inputs, from Universal Resource Locator (URL) parameters to Hypertext Transfer Protocol (HTTP) POST content and, more recently, Extensible Markup Language (XML) content in the form of Web service messages. Different active content technologies have different associated vulnerabilities, and their risks should be weighed against their benefits. Although most Web sites use some form of active content generators, many also deliver some or all of their content in a non-active form.

Organizations must use authentication and cryptographic technologies as appropriate to protect certain types of sensitive data.

Public Web servers often support a range of technologies for identifying and authenticating users with differing privileges for accessing information. Some of these technologies are based on cryptographic functions that can provide an encrypted channel between a Web browser client and a Web server that supports encryption. Web servers may be configured to use different cryptographic algorithms, providing varying levels of security and performance.

Without proper user authentication in place, organizations cannot selectively restrict access to specific information. All information that resides on a public Web server is then accessible by anyone with access to the server. In addition, without some process to authenticate the server, users of the public Web server will not be able to determine whether the server is the "authentic" Web server or a counterfeit version operated by a malicious entity.

Even with an encrypted channel and an authentication mechanism, it is possible that attackers may attempt to access the site via a brute force attack. Improper authentication techniques can allow attackers to gather valid usernames or potentially gain access to the Web site. Strong authentication mechanisms can also protect against phishing and pharming attacks. Therefore, an appropriate level of authentication should be implemented based on the sensitivity of the Web server's users and content.

Organizations should employ their network infrastructure to help protect their public Web servers.

The network infrastructure (e.g., firewalls, routers, IDSs) that supports the Web server plays a critical role in the security of the Web server. In most configurations, the network infrastructure will be the first line of defense between a public Web server and the Internet. Network design alone, however, cannot protect a Web server. The frequency, sophistication, and variety of Web server attacks perpetrated today support the idea that Web server security must be implemented through layered and diverse protection mechanisms (i.e., defense-in-depth).

Organizations should commit to the ongoing process of maintaining the security of public Web servers to ensure continued security.

Maintaining a secure Web server requires constant effort, resources, and vigilance from an organization. Securely administering a Web server on a daily basis is an essential aspect of Web server security. Maintaining the security of a Web server will usually involve the following steps:

- Configuring, protecting, and analyzing log files

- Backing up critical information frequently

- Maintaining a protected authoritative copy of the organization's Web content

- Establishing and following procedures for recovering from compromise

- Testing and applying patches in a timely manner

- Testing security periodically.

1. Introduction

1.1 Authority

The National Institute of Standards and Technology (NIST) developed this document in furtherance of its statutory responsibilities under the Federal Information Security Management Act (FISMA) of 2002, Public Law 107-347.

NIST is responsible for developing standards and guidelines, including minimum requirements, for providing adequate information security for all agency operations and assets; but such standards and guidelines shall not apply to national security systems. This guideline is consistent with the requirements of the Office of Management and Budget (OMB) Circular A-130, Section 8b(3), "Securing Agency Information Systems," as analyzed in A-130, Appendix IV: Analysis of Key Sections. Supplemental information is provided in A-130, Appendix III.

This guideline has been prepared for use by Federal agencies. It may be used by nongovernmental organizations on a voluntary basis and is not subject to copyright, although attribution is desired.

Nothing in this document should be taken to contradict standards and guidelines made mandatory and binding on Federal agencies by the Secretary of Commerce under statutory authority, nor should these guidelines be interpreted as altering or superseding the existing authorities of the Secretary of Commerce, the Director of the OMB, or any other Federal official.

1.2 Purpose and Scope

The purpose of the *Guidelines on Securing Public Web Servers* is to recommend security practices for designing, implementing, and operating publicly accessible Web servers, including related network infrastructure issues. Some Federal organizations might need to go beyond these recommendations or adapt them in other ways to meet their unique requirements. While intended as recommendations for Federal departments and agencies, it may be used in the private sector on a voluntary basis.

This document may be used by organizations interested in enhancing security on existing and future Web server systems to reduce the number and frequency of Web-related security incidents. This document presents generic principles that apply to all systems.

This guideline does not cover the following aspects relating to securing a Web server:

- Securing other types of network servers

- Firewalls and routers used to protect Web servers beyond a basic discussion in Section 8

- Security considerations related to Web client (browser) software[4]

- Special considerations for high-traffic Web sites with multiple hosts[5]

- Securing back-end servers that may support the Web server (e.g., database servers, file servers)

---

[4]   For more information on securing Web browsers, see NIST Special Publication (SP) 800-46, *Security for Telecommuting and Broadband Communications* (http://csrc.nist.gov/publications/nistpubs/).

[5]   Although this document does not address the specific security concerns that arise from high-traffic multiple-server Web farms, much of what is covered will apply to these types of installations.

- Services other than Hypertext Transfer Protocol (HTTP) and Hypertext Transfer Protocol Secure (HTTPS)

- SOAP-style Web Services[6]

- Protection of intellectual property.

1.3   Audience and Assumptions

This document, while technical in nature, provides the background information to help readers understand the topics that are discussed. The intended audience for this document includes the following:

- System engineers and architects, when designing and implementing Web servers

- Web and system administrators, when administering, patching, securing, or upgrading Web servers

- Webmasters, when creating and managing Web content

- Security consultants, when performing security audits to determine information system (IS) security postures

- Program managers and information technology (IT) security officers, to ensure that adequate security measures have been considered for all phases of the system's life cycle.

This document assumes that readers have some minimal operating system, networking, and Web server expertise. Because of the constantly changing nature of Web server threats and vulnerabilities, readers are expected to take advantage of other resources (including those listed in this document) for more current and detailed information.

The practices recommended in this document are designed to help mitigate the risks associated with Web servers. They build on and assume the implementation of practices described in other NIST guidelines listed in Appendix E.

1.4   Document Structure

The remainder of this document is organized into the following eight major sections:

- Section 2 discusses Web server security problems and presents an overview.

- Section 3 discusses the planning and management of Web servers.

- Section 4 presents an overview of securing the underlying operating system for a Web server.

- Section 5 discusses securely installing and configuring a Web server.

- Section 6 examines the security of Web content.

- Section 7 examines popular Web authentication and encryption technologies.

---

[6]   NIST SP 800-95, *Guide to Secure Web Services*, provides insight into the risks introduced by Web services and how to mitigate them (http://csrc.nist.gov/publications/nistpubs/).

■ Section 8 discusses protecting a Web server through the supporting network infrastructure.

■ Section 9 discusses the basics of securely administering a Web server on a daily basis.

The document also contains several appendices with supporting material.

■ Appendix A provides a variety of online Web security resources.

■ Appendix B defines terms used in this document.

■ Appendix C provides a list of commonly used Web server security tools and applications.

■ Appendix D lists references used in this document.

■ Appendix E provides a Web server security checklist.

■ Appendix F contains an acronym list.

■ Appendix G contains an index for the publication.

2. Background

The World Wide Web is one of the most important ways for an organization to publish information, interact with Internet users, and establish an e-commerce/e-government presence. However, if an organization is not rigorous in configuring and operating its public Web site, it may be vulnerable to a variety of security threats. Although the threats in cyberspace remain largely the same as in the physical world (e.g., fraud, theft, vandalism, and terrorism), they are far more dangerous as a result of three important developments: increased efficiency, action at a distance, and rapid technique propagation [Schn00].

■ **Increased Efficiency**—Automation makes attacks, even those with minimal opportunity for success, efficient and extremely profitable. For example, in the physical world, an attack that would succeed once in 10,000 attempts would be ineffectual because of the time and effort required, on average, for a single success. The time invested in achieving a single success would be outweighed by the time invested in the 9,999 failures. On the Internet, automation enables the same attack to be a stunning success. Computing power and bandwidth are becoming less expensive daily, while the number of hosts that can be targeted is growing rapidly. This synergy means that almost any attack, no matter how low its success rate, will likely find many systems to exploit.

■ **Action at a Distance**—The Internet allows action at a distance. The Internet has no borders, and every point on the Internet is potentially reachable from every other point. This means that an attacker in one country can target a remote Web site in another country as easily as one close to home.

■ **Rapid Technique Propagation**—The Internet allows for easier and more rapid technique propagation. Before the Internet, techniques for attack were developed that would take years, if ever, to propagate, allowing time to develop effective countermeasures. Today, a new technique can be propagated within hours or days. It is now more difficult to develop effective countermeasures in a timely manner.

Compromised Web sites have served as an entry point for intrusions into many organizations' internal networks. Organizations can face monetary losses, damage to reputation, or legal action if an intruder successfully violates the confidentiality of their data. Denial of service (DoS) attacks can make it difficult, if not impossible, for users to access an organization's Web site.[7] These attacks may cost the organization significant time and money. DoS attacks are easy for attackers to attempt because of the number of possible attack vectors, the variety of automated tools available, and the low skill level needed to use the tools. DoS attacks, as well as threats of initiating DoS attacks, are also increasingly being used to blackmail organizations. In addition, an organization can find itself in an embarrassing situation resulting from malicious intruders changing the content of the organization's Web pages.

Kossakowski and Allen identified three main security issues related to the operation of a publicly accessible Web site [Koss00]:

■ Misconfiguration or other improper operation of the Web server, which may result, for example, in the disclosure or alteration of proprietary or sensitive information. This information can include items such as the following:

---

[7] Many DoS attacks are a result of botnets, a group of computers with a program surreptitiously installed to cause them to attack other systems. Botnets are often composed primarily of poorly secured home computers that have high-speed Internet connectivity. Botnets can be used to perform distributed denial of service (DDoS) attacks, which are much harder to defend against because of the large number of attacking hosts.

- Assets of the organization

- Configuration of the server or network that could be exploited for subsequent attacks

- Information regarding the users or administrator(s) of the Web server, including their passwords.

- Vulnerabilities within the Web server that might allow, for example, attackers to compromise the security of the server and other hosts on the organization's network by taking actions such as the following:

  - Defacing the Web site or otherwise affect information integrity

  - Executing unauthorized commands or programs on the host operating system, including ones that the intruder has installed

  - Gaining unauthorized access to resources elsewhere in the organization's computer network

  - Launching attacks on external sites from the Web server, thus concealing the intruders' identities, and perhaps making the organization liable for damages

  - Using the server as a distribution point for illegally copied software, attack tools, or pornography, perhaps making the organization liable for damages

  - Using the server to deliver attacks against vulnerable Web clients to compromise them.

- Inadequate or unavailable defense mechanisms for the Web server to prevent certain classes of attacks, such as DoS attacks, which disrupt the availability of the Web server and prevent authorized users from accessing the Web site when required.

In recent years, as the security of networks and server installations have improved, poorly written software applications and scripts that allow attackers to compromise the security of the Web server or collect data from backend databases have become the targets of attacks. Many dynamic Web applications do not perform sufficient validation of user input, allowing attackers to submit commands that are run on the server. Common examples of this form of attack are structured query language (SQL) injection, where an attacker submits input that will be passed to a database and processed, and cross-site scripting, where an attacker manipulates the application to store scripting language commands that are activated when another user accesses the Web page.

A number of steps are required to ensure the security of any public Web server. As a prerequisite for taking any step, however, it is essential that the organization have a security policy in place. Taking the following steps within the context of the organization's security policy should prove effective:

- Step 1: Installing, configuring, and securing the underlying operating system (OS)

- Step 2: Installing, configuring, and securing Web server software

- Step 3: Employing appropriate network protection mechanisms (e.g., firewall, packet filtering router, and proxy)

- Step 4: Ensuring that any applications developed specifically for the Web server are coded following secure programming practices

■ Step 5: Maintaining the secure configuration through application of appropriate patches and upgrades, security testing, monitoring of logs, and backups of data and OS

■ Step 6: Using, publicizing, and protecting information and data in a careful and systemic manner

■ Step 7: Employing secure administration and maintenance processes (including server/application updating and log reviews)

■ Step 8: Conducting initial and periodic vulnerability scans of each public Web server and supporting network infrastructure (e.g., firewalls, routers).

The practices recommended in this document are designed to help mitigate the risks associated with public Web servers. They build on and assume the implementation of practices described in the NIST publications on system and network security listed in Appendix A.

When addressing Web server security issues, it is an excellent idea to keep in mind the following general information security principles [Curt01 and Salt75]:

■ **Simplicity**—Security mechanisms (and information systems in general) should be as simple as possible. Complexity is at the root of many security issues.

■ **Fail-Safe**—If a failure occurs, the system should fail in a secure manner, i.e., security controls and settings remain in effect and are enforced. It is usually better to lose functionality rather than security.

■ **Complete Mediation**—Rather than providing direct access to information, mediators that enforce access policy should be employed. Common examples of mediators include file system permissions, proxies, firewalls, and mail gateways.

■ **Open Design**—System security should not depend on the secrecy of the implementation or its components. "Security through obscurity" is not reliable.

■ **Separation of Privilege**—Functions, to the degree possible, should be separate and provide as much granularity as possible. The concept can apply to both systems and operators and users. In the case of systems, functions such as read, edit, write, and execute should be separate. In the case of system operators and users, roles should be as separate as possible. For example, if resources allow, the role of system administrator should be separate from that of the security administrator.

■ **Least Privilege**—This principle dictates that each task, process, or user is granted the minimum rights required to perform its job. By applying this principle consistently, if a task, process, or user is compromised, the scope of damage is constrained to the limited resources available to the compromised entity.

■ **Psychological Acceptability**—Users should understand the necessity of security. This can be provided through training and education. In addition, the security mechanisms in place should present users with sensible options that give them the usability they require on a daily basis. If users find the security mechanisms too cumbersome, they may devise ways to work around or compromise them. The objective is not to weaken security so it is understandable and acceptable, but to train and educate users and to design security mechanisms and policies that are usable and effective.

- **Least Common Mechanism**—When providing a feature for the system, it is best to have a single process or service gain some function without granting that same function to other parts of the system. The ability for the Web server process to access a back-end database, for instance, should not also enable other applications on the system to access the back-end database.

- **Defense-in-Depth**—Organizations should understand that a single security mechanism is generally insufficient. Security mechanisms (defenses) need to be layered so that compromise of a single security mechanism is insufficient to compromise a host or network. No "silver bullet" exists for information system security.

- **Work Factor**—Organizations should understand what it would take to break the system or network's security features. The amount of work necessary for an attacker to break the system or network should exceed the value that the attacker would gain from a successful compromise.

- **Compromise Recording**—Records and logs should be maintained so that if a compromise does occur, evidence of the attack is available to the organization. This information can assist in securing the network and host after the compromise and aid in identifying the methods and exploits used by the attacker. This information can be used to better secure the host or network in the future. In addition, these records and logs can assist organizations in identifying and prosecuting attackers.

3. Planning and Managing Web Servers

The most critical aspect of deploying a secure Web server is careful planning prior to installation, configuration, and deployment. Careful planning will ensure that the Web server is as secure as possible and in compliance with all relevant organizational policies. Many Web server security and performance problems can be traced to a lack of planning or management controls. The importance of management controls cannot be overstated. In many organizations, the IT support structure is highly fragmented. This fragmentation leads to inconsistencies, and these inconsistencies can lead to security vulnerabilities and other issues.

3.1 Installation and Deployment Planning

Security should be considered from the initial planning stage at the beginning of the systems development life cycle to maximize security and minimize costs. It is much more difficult and expensive to address security after deployment and implementation. Organizations are more likely to make decisions about configuring hosts appropriately and consistently if they begin by developing and using a detailed, well-designed deployment plan. Developing such a plan enables organizations to make informed tradeoff decisions between usability and performance, and risk. A deployment plan allows organizations to maintain secure configurations and aids in identifying security vulnerabilities, which often manifest themselves as deviations from the plan.

In the planning stages of a Web server, the following items should be considered [Alle00]:

- Identify the purpose(s) of the Web server.

  - What information categories will be stored on the Web server?

  - What information categories will be processed on or transmitted through the Web server?

  - What are the security requirements for this information?

  - Will any information be retrieved from or stored on another host (e.g., back-end database, mail server)?

  - What are the security requirements for any other hosts involved (e.g., back-end database, directory server, mail server, proxy server)?

  - What other service(s) will be provided by the Web server (in general, dedicating the host to being only a Web server is the most secure option)?

  - What are the security requirements for these additional services?

  - What are the requirements for continuity of services provided by Web servers, such as those specified in continuity of operations plans and disaster recovery plans?

  - Where on the network will the Web server be located (see Section 8)?

- Identify the network services that will be provided on the Web server, such as those supplied through the following protocols:

  - HTTP

- HTTPS[8]

- Internet Caching Protocol (ICP)

- Hyper Text Caching Protocol (HTCP)

- Web Cache Coordination Protocol (WCCP)

- SOCKS[9]

- Database services (e.g., Open Database Connectivity [ODBC]).

■ Identify any network service software, both client and server, to be installed on the Web server and any other support servers.

■ Identify the users or categories of users of the Web server and any support hosts.

■ Determine the privileges that each category of user will have on the Web server and support hosts.

■ Determine how the Web server will be managed (e.g., locally, remotely from the internal network, remotely from external networks).

■ Decide if and how users will be authenticated and how authentication data will be protected.

■ Determine how appropriate access to information resources will be enforced.

■ Determine which Web server applications meet the organization's requirements. Consider servers that may offer greater security, albeit with less functionality in some instances. Some issues to consider include—

- Cost

- Compatibility with existing infrastructure

- Knowledge of existing employees

- Existing manufacturer relationship

- Past vulnerability history

- Functionality.

■ Work closely with manufacturer(s) in the planning stage.

The choice of Web server application may determine the choice of OS. However, to the degree possible, Web server administrators should choose an OS that provides the following [Alle00]:

■ Ability to restrict administrative or root level activities to authorized users only

---

[8]   HTTP transactions protected via the Secure Sockets Layer (SSL)/Transport Layer Security (TLS) protocols (see Section 7).
[9]   "SOCKS" is an abbreviation for "SOCKetS".

■ Ability to control access to data on the server

■ Ability to disable unnecessary network services that may be built into the OS or server software

■ Ability to control access to various forms of executable programs, such as Common Gateway Interface (CGI) scripts and server plug-ins in the case of Web servers

■ Ability to log appropriate server activities to detect intrusions and attempted intrusions

■ Provision of a host-based firewall capability.

In addition, organizations should consider the availability of trained, experienced staff to administer the server and server products. Many organizations have learned the difficult lesson that a capable and experienced administrator for one type of operating environment is not automatically as effective for another.

Although many Web servers do not host sensitive information, most Web servers should be considered sensitive because of the damage to the organization's reputation that could occur if the servers' integrity is compromised. In such cases, it is critical that the Web servers are located in areas that provide secure physical environments. When planning the location of a Web server, the following issues should be considered:

■ Are the appropriate physical security protection mechanisms in place? Examples include—

  ■ Locks

  ■ Card reader access

  ■ Security guards

  ■ Physical IDSs (e.g., motion sensors, cameras).

■ Are there appropriate environmental controls so that the necessary humidity and temperature are maintained?

■ Is there a backup power source? For how long will it provide power?

■ If high availability is required, are there redundant Internet connections from at least two different Internet service providers (ISP)?

■ If the location is subject to known natural disasters, is it hardened against those disasters and/or is there a contingency site outside the potential disaster area?

3.2   Security Management Staff

Because Web server security is tightly intertwined with the organization's general information system security posture, a number of IT and system security staff may be interested in Web server planning, implementation, and administration. This section provides a list of generic roles and identifies their responsibilities as they relate to Web server security. These roles are for the purpose of discussion and may vary by organization.

3.2.1 Senior IT Management/Chief Information Officer

The Senior IT Management/Chief Information Officer (CIO) ensures that the organization's security posture is adequate. The Senior IT Management provides direction and advisory services for the protection of information systems for the entire organization. The Senior IT Management/CIO is responsible for the following activities associated with Web servers:

- Coordinating the development and maintenance of the organization's information security policies, standards, and procedures

- Coordinating the development and maintenance of the organization's change control and management procedures

- Ensuring the establishment of, and compliance with, consistent IT security policies for departments throughout the organization

- Coordinating with upper management, public affairs, and other relevant personnel to produce a formal policy and process for publishing information to Web sites and ensuring this policy is enforced.

3.2.2 Information Systems Security Program Managers

The Information Systems Security Program Managers (ISSPM) oversee the implementation of and compliance with the standards, rules, and regulations specified in the organization's security policy. The ISSPMs are responsible for the following activities associated with Web servers:

- Ensuring that security procedures are developed and implemented

- Ensuring that security policies, standards, and requirements are followed

- Ensuring that all critical systems are identified and that contingency planning, disaster recovery plans, and continuity of operations plans exist for these critical systems

- Ensuring that critical systems are identified and scheduled for periodic security testing according to the security policy requirements of each respective system.

3.2.3 Information Systems Security Officers

Information Systems Security Officers (ISSO) are responsible for overseeing all aspects of information security within a specific organizational entity. They ensure that the organization's information security practices comply with organizational and departmental policies, standards, and procedures. ISSOs are responsible for the following activities associated with Web servers:

- Developing internal security standards and procedures for the Web server(s) and supporting network infrastructure

- Cooperating in the development and implementation of security tools, mechanisms, and mitigation techniques

- Maintaining standard configuration profiles of the Web servers and supporting network infrastructure controlled by the organization, including, but not limited to, OSs, firewalls, routers, and Web server applications

■ Maintaining operational integrity of systems by conducting security tests and ensuring that designated IT professionals are conducting scheduled testing on critical systems.

3.2.4 Web Server and Network Administrators

Web server administrators are system architects responsible for the overall design, implementation, and maintenance of a Web server. Network administrators are responsible for the overall design, implementation, and maintenance of a network. On a daily basis, Web server and network administrators contend with the security requirements of the specific system(s) for which they are responsible. Security issues and solutions can originate from either outside (e.g., security patches and fixes from the manufacturer or computer security incident response teams) or within the organization (e.g., the security office). The administrators are responsible for the following activities associated with Web servers:

■ Installing and configuring systems in compliance with the organizational security policies and standard system and network configurations

■ Maintaining systems in a secure manner, including frequent backups and timely application of patches

■ Monitoring system integrity, protection levels, and security-related events

■ Following up on detected security anomalies associated with their information system resources

■ Conducting security tests as required.

3.2.5 Web Application Developers

Web application developers are responsible for the look, functionality, performance, and security of the Web content and Web-based applications they create. As mentioned in Section 2, threats are increasingly directed at applications instead of the underlying Web server software and OSs. Unless Web application developers ensure that their code takes security into consideration, the Web server's security will be weak no matter how well the server itself and the supporting infrastructure are secured. Web application developers should ensure the applications they implement have the following characteristics:

■ Supports a secure authentication, authorization, and access control mechanism as required.

■ Performs input validation so that the application's security mechanisms cannot be bypassed when a malicious user tampers with data he or she sends to the application, including HTTP requests, headers, query strings, cookies, form fields, and hidden fields.

■ Processes errors in a secure manner so as not to lead to exposure of sensitive implementation information.

■ Protects sensitive information processed and/or stored by the application. Inadequate protection can allow data tampering and access to confidential information such as usernames, passwords, and credit card numbers.

■ Maintains its own application-specific logs. In many instances, Web server logging is not sufficient to track what a user does at the application level, requiring the application to maintain its own logs. Insufficient logging details can lead to a lack of knowledge about possible intrusions and an inability to verify a user's actions (both legitimate and malicious).

■ Is "hardened" against application-level DoS attacks. Although DoS attacks are most frequently targeted at the network and transport layers, the application itself can be a target. If a malicious user can monopolize a required application or system resource, legitimate users can be prevented from using the system.

3.3 Management Practices

Appropriate management practices are critical to operating and maintaining a secure Web server. Security practices entail the identification of an organization's information system assets and the development, documentation, and implementation of policies, standards, procedures, and guidelines that ensure confidentiality, integrity, and availability of information system resources.

To ensure the security of a Web server and the supporting network infrastructure, organizations should implement the following practices:

■ **Organizational Information System Security Policy**—A security policy should specify the basic information system security tenets and rules, and their intended internal purpose. The policy should also outline who in the organization is responsible for particular areas of information security (e.g., implementation, enforcement, audit, review). The policy must be enforced consistently throughout the organization to be effective. Generally, the CIO and senior management are responsible for drafting the organization's security policy.

■ **Configuration/Change Control and Management**—The process of controlling modification to a system's design, hardware, firmware, and software provides sufficient assurance that the system is protected against the introduction of an improper modification before, during, and after system implementation. Configuration control leads to consistency with the organization's information system security policy. Configuration control is traditionally overseen by a configuration control board that is the final authority on all proposed changes to an information system. If resources allow, consider the use of development, quality assurance, and/or test environments so that changes can be vetted and tested before deployment in production.

■ **Risk Assessment and Management**—Risk assessment is the process of analyzing and interpreting risk. It involves determining an assessment's scope and methodology, collecting and analyzing risk-related data, and interpreting the risk analysis results. Collecting and analyzing risk data requires identifying assets, threats, vulnerabilities, safeguards, consequences, and the probability of a successful attack. Risk management is the process of selecting and implementing controls to reduce risk to a level acceptable to the organization.

■ **Standardized Configurations**—Organizations should develop standardized secure configurations for widely used OSs and applications. This will provide recommendations to Web server and network administrators on how to configure their systems securely and ensure consistency and compliance with the organizational security policy. Because it only takes one insecurely configured host to compromise a network, organizations with a significant number of hosts are especially encouraged to apply this recommendation.

■ **Secure Programming Practices**—Organizations should adopt secure application development guidelines to ensure that they develop their Web applications in a sufficiently secure manner.

■ **Security Awareness and Training**—A security training program is critical to the overall security posture of an organization. Making users and administrators aware of their security responsibilities and teaching the correct practices helps them change their behavior to conform to security best practices. Training also supports individual accountability, which is an important method for improving information system security. If the user community includes members of the general public, providing security awareness specifically targeting them might also be appropriate.

■ **Contingency, Continuity of Operations, and Disaster Recovery Planning**—Contingency plans, continuity of operations plans, and disaster recovery plans are established in advance to allow an organization or facility to maintain operations in the event of a disruption.[10]

■ **Certification and Accreditation**—Certification in the context of information systems security means that a system has been analyzed to determine how well it meets all of the security requirements of the organization. Accreditation occurs when the organization's management accepts that the system meets the organization's security requirements.[11]

3.4 System Security Plan

The objective of system security planning is to improve protection of information system resources.[12] Plans that adequately protect information assets require managers and information owners—directly affected by and interested in the information and/or processing capabilities—to be convinced that their information assets are adequately protected from loss, misuse, unauthorized access or modification, unavailability, and undetected activities.

The purpose of the system security plan is to provide an overview of the security and privacy requirements of the system and describe the controls in place or planned for meeting those requirements. The system security plan also delineates responsibilities and expected behavior of all individuals who access the system. The system security plan should be viewed as documentation of the structured process of planning adequate, cost-effective security protection for a system. It should reflect input from various managers with responsibilities concerning the system, including information owners, the system owner, and the ISSPM.

For Federal agencies, all information systems must be covered by a system security plan. Other organizations should strongly consider the completion of a system security plan for each of their systems as well. The information system owner[13] is generally the party responsible for ensuring that the security plan is developed and maintained and that the system is deployed and operated according to the agreed-upon security requirements.

In general, an effective system security plan should include the following:

■ **System Identification**—The first sections of the system security plan provide basic identifying information about the system. They contain general information such as the key points of contact for the system, the purpose of the system, the sensitivity level of the system, and the environment in which the system is deployed.

---

[10] For more information, see NIST SP 800-34, *Contingency Planning Guide for Information Technology Systems* (http://csrc.nist.gov/publications/nistpubs/).

[11] For more information on certification and accreditation, see NIST SP 800-37, *Federal Guidelines for the Security Certification and Accreditation of Information Technology Systems* (http://csrc.nist.gov/publications/nistpubs/).

[12] For more information on system security plans, see NIST SP 800-18 Revision 1, *Guide for Developing Security Plans for Federal Information Systems* (http://csrc.nist.gov/publications/nistpubs/).

[13] The information system owner is responsible for defining the system's operating parameters, authorized functions, and security requirements. The information owner for information stored within, processed by, or transmitted by a system may or may not be the same as the information system owner. In addition, a single system may use information from multiple information owners.

■ **Controls**—This section of the plan describes the control measures (in place or planned) that are intended to meet the protection requirements of the information system. Controls fall into three general categories:

■ Management controls, which focus on the management of the computer security system and the management of risk for a system.

■ Operational controls, which are primary implemented and executed by people (rather than systems). They often require technical or specialized expertise, and often rely upon management activities as well as technical controls.

■ Technical controls, which are security mechanisms that the computer system employs. The controls can provide automated protection from unauthorized access or misuse, facilitate detection of security violations, and support security requirements for applications and data. The implementation of technical controls, however, always requires significant operational considerations and should be consistent with the management of security within the organization [NIST06a]. [14]

3.5 Human Resources Requirements

The greatest challenge and expense in developing and securely maintaining a public Web server is providing the necessary human resources to adequately perform the required functions. Many organizations fail to fully recognize the amount of expense and skills required to field a secure public Web server. This failure often results in overworked employees and insecure systems. From the initial planning stages, organizations need to determine the necessary human resource requirements. Appropriate and sufficient human resources are the single most important aspect of effective Web server security. Organizations should also consider the fact that, in general, technical solutions are not a substitute for skilled and experienced personnel.

When considering the human resource implications of developing and deploying a Web server, organizations should consider the following:

■ **Required Personnel**—What types of personnel are required? This would include such positions as system and Web server administrators, Webmasters, network administrators, and ISSOs.

■ **Required Skills**—What are the required skills to adequately plan, develop, and maintain the Web server in a secure manner? Examples include OS administration, network administration, active content expertise, and programming.

■ **Available Personnel**—What are the available human resources within the organization? In addition, what are their current skill sets and are they sufficient for supporting the Web server? Often, an organization discovers that its existing human resources are not sufficient and needs to consider the following options:

■ Train Current Staff—If there are personnel available but they do not have the requisite skills, the organization may choose to train the existing staff in the skills required. Although this is an excellent option, the organization should ensure that employees meet all prerequisites for training.

---

[14] For more detail on management, operational, and technical controls, see NIST SP 800-53 Revision 1, *Recommended Security Controls for Federal Information Systems*, and NIST SP 800-100, *Information Security Handbook: A Guide for Managers* (http://csrc.nist.gov/publications/nistpubs/).

- Acquire Additional Staff—If there are not enough staff members available or they do not have the requisite skills, it may be necessary to hire additional personnel or use external resources.

Once the organization has staffed the project and the Web server is active, it will be necessary to ensure the number and skills of the personnel are still adequate. The threat and vulnerability levels of IT systems, including Web servers, are constantly changing, as is the technology. This means that what is adequate today may not be tomorrow.

3.6 Alternative Web Server Platforms

Although many organizations manage Web servers that operate over general-purpose OSs, there are instances in which an organization may wish to use one of the alternatives discussed below. Although these technologies are relatively new to the area of Web servers, they are based on sound technologies and have started to see broader use in the Web server environment.

3.6.1 Trusted Operating Systems

Trusted operating systems (TOS) are security-modified or -enhanced OSs that include additional security mechanisms not found in most general-purpose OSs. They were originally created to meet the need of the Federal government for high security mandatory access control (MAC) systems. TOSs provide a very secure system-wide control policy, a finely defined set of access privileges, and extensive logging and auditing capabilities. Many TOSs are independently verified to ensure that they meet the requirements set forth in their design documentation.

TOSs are generally used in applications for which security is paramount. TOSs can securely control all aspects of a computing environment, including networking resources, users, processes, and memory. Specifically, TOSs can limit access to system resources in a manner that is not likely to be interfered with or compromised.

Using a TOS will generally produce a very secure Web server; however, some difficulties exist in using TOSs. A major drawback is that configuring and administering a TOS requires knowledge of each protected subsystem and its access needs. It may also require significant planning and administrative overhead to design and support a complex Web site on a TOS. However, even with these limitations, organizations that have very high security requirements should consider using a TOS on their Web servers.

Some manufacturers have begun bundling their OS offerings with most or all of the functionality of traditional TOSs for use in server or workstation environments. Organizations may benefit from such systems because much of the overhead in designing and configuring the Web server to run in a TOS environment has been performed by the manufacturer. Web servers benefit from the TOS' MAC in that the system can explicitly deny the Web server process access to sensitive portions of the system even if an attacker has managed to take control of the process.

The following are some issues to keep in mind when considering a Web platform:

- What is the underlying OS and how has it fared in security testing?

- Does the organization have the necessary expertise in administering a TOS?

- Are the additional costs of purchasing and supporting a TOS outweighed by the benefits?

■ Is the TOS compatible with the organization's existing Web applications and scripts?

■ Is the TOS compatible with the organization's other applications and servers with which it will be interoperating?

3.6.2 Web Server Appliances

A Web server appliance is a software/hardware combination that is designed to be a "plug-and-play" Web server. These appliances employ the use of a simplified OS that is optimized to support a Web server. The simplified OS improves security by minimizing unnecessary features, services, and options. The Web server application on these systems is often pre-hardened and pre-configured for security.

These systems offer other benefits in addition to security. Performance is often enhanced because the system (i.e., OS, Web server application, and hardware) is designed and built specifically to operate as a Web server. Cost is often reduced because hardware and software not specifically required by a Web server are not included. These systems can be an excellent option for small- to medium-size organizations that cannot afford a full-time Web administrator.

The greatest weakness in these systems is that they may not be suitable for large, complex, and multi-layered Web sites. They may be limited in what types of active content they support (e.g., J2EE, .NET, PHP Hypertext Preprocessor [PHP]), potentially reducing the options available to an organization. An appliance may host the back-end database as well as the front-end Web interface, potentially preventing organizations from having separate servers for each. Finally, it may be difficult to configure appliances from different manufacturers to work together. Nevertheless, because they offer a secure environment and an easy-to-configure interface, small- to medium-size organizations may find appliances an attractive option requiring less administrative effort. Web server appliances are available from most major hardware manufacturers and from various specialized manufacturers that concentrate solely on Web server appliances.

In addition to Web server appliances, there are also a growing number of security appliances available for Web servers. These systems augment the security mechanisms on the Web server itself. In some cases, these systems can prevent attacks from reaching a Web server, which is especially helpful if the server has known vulnerabilities (e.g., new patches have not yet been applied). The most common types of security appliances are—

■ Secure Sockets Layer (SSL) accelerators, which off-load the computationally expensive processing required for initiating SSL/Transport Layer Security (TLS) connections

■ Security gateways, which monitor HTTP traffic to and from the Web server for potential attacks and take action as necessary

■ Content filters, which can monitor traffic to and from the Web server for potentially sensitive or inappropriate data and take action as necessary

■ Authentication gateways, which authenticate users via a variety of authentication mechanisms and control access to Universal Resource Locators (URL) hosted on the Web server itself.

In many instances, most or all of the above-mentioned functionality is combined in a single device, which is frequently referred to as a reverse proxy.[15]

In organizations requiring complicated dynamic Web sites, the security appliance configuration may be complex, which could cause configuration errors that reduce the effectiveness of the appliance. It is important to practice defense-in-depth to ensure that any vulnerabilities present in the security appliance or its configuration do not adversely affect the organization as a whole.

An additional challenge presented by appliance devices is that they often employ commonly used open-source software. This is normally not a problem, but it can become one when a vulnerability is found in the underlying software because it is frequently not possible to use the patch released by the open-source software group. Common reasons for this inability to use the patch include possible violations of the licensing or support agreements with the appliance manufacturer, and technical problems in applying updates to the appliance (e.g., administrators often do not have OS-level access to appliances). Therefore, appliances can be open to attack for a longer period of time than non-appliance systems because of the additional delay involved in appliance manufacturers developing, testing, and releasing patches. Another possible problem with appliances is that they usually do not allow the installation of additional software for administration or for security, such as antivirus software or host-based intrusion detection agents.

The following are some issues to consider when contemplating the purchase of a Web appliance:

■ What is the underlying OS and how has it fared in security testing?

■ How has the appliance itself fared in security testing? (Note that the configuration options of Web appliances are necessarily limited, so a Web appliance will generally only be as secure as its default installation configuration.)

■ How heterogeneous is the organization's Web server infrastructure? (Different brands of appliances may not work well together.)

■ Are the expansion options inherent in the appliance acceptable to the organization? (Organizations that are anticipating or experiencing rapid growth in Web traffic may not want to limit themselves to a single appliance or appliance vendor.)

■ How difficult is it to configure the appliance? Is the appliance flexible enough to meet the organization's needs?

■ How quickly does the manufacturer respond to and provide patches for potential vulnerabilities?

■ Is the underlying software used on the appliance proprietary, open source, or a combination of both?

■ How long will the manufacturer support the appliance and what is the manufacturer's history of support for legacy appliances?

3.6.3 Pre-Hardened Operating Systems and Web Servers

A growing number of pre-hardened OS and Web server packages are being distributed today. These packages include an OS and Web server application that are modified and pre-configured to provide high security. Some of these packages include the hardware platform, while others are software distributions

---

[15] This is not meant to imply that all reverse proxies are appliance-based; in fact, many are not.

that include only the OS and Web server application. These distributions are generally based on hardened and/or modified general-purpose OSs (e.g., Linux, Unix, Windows) that are specifically designed to support a secure Web server. The Web server application is also often based on a hardened and/or modified generally available Web server application (e.g., Apache, Internet Information Service [IIS]). These packages often include a greater number of security options and are designed to be easier to configure through the use of precompiled scripts and graphical user interfaces (GUI). Although each of these packages is different, they usually rely on one or more of the following to provide a higher level of protection and security:

- Secure initial default configuration

- Hardened OS or TOS

- Hardened Web server software

- Extensive auditing capabilities

- Application wrappers

- Network wrappers and/or host-based firewall capabilities

- Host-based IDSs

- Simplified security administration (e.g., menus, GUIs).

These types of systems should be considered by organizations that face a significant threat level and/or have high-value Web sites (e.g., major Federal government organizations, banks, health insurance companies). These packages are available from some major hardware and software manufacturers in addition to various specialized manufacturers.

Some issues to consider when contemplating the purchase of a hardened Web appliance:

- What is the underlying OS and how has it fared in security testing?

- How has the Web server application itself fared in security testing?

- How difficult is it to administer?

- Are the hardened Web server application and OS compatible with the organization's existing Web applications and scripts?

- How quickly does the manufacturer respond to and provide patches for potential vulnerabilities?

3.6.4 Virtualized Platforms

Virtual machine technology is being used more and more frequently for Web servers. Through virtualization, a single physical host computer can run multiple virtual machines, each with a distinct guest OS and associated applications. A guest OS need not be aware of other OSs—even that of the supporting host—running on the same physical platform. Virtual machine technology is improving constantly. New versions of mainstream OSs are being designed with virtualization in mind and new x86 64-bit processors provide hardware-level support for virtualization.

Virtualization allows organizations to reduce costs by running multiple Web servers on a single host computer and by providing a mechanism for quickly responding to attacks against a Web server. The list below defines the three main types of virtual machine technology. Note that some virtualization software may be a hybrid implementation, depending on the hardware and guest OSs.

- Full virtualization, which simulates all of the hardware required by the guest OS. Full virtualization is useful in situations where the guest OS runs on a different machine architecture than the host. Full virtualization results in a significant performance hit because all commands must be emulated by software.

- Native virtualization, which simulates only the hardware necessary to run an unmodified guest OS. In native virtualization, most commands can be passed unmodified to the host computer processing unit (CPU), which reduces the performance hit.

- Paravirtualization, which does not simulate hardware. Instead, it offers an application programming interface (API) that can be used by a modified guest OS, or it takes advantage of virtualization capabilities supported by the processor.

Virtualization adds another layer of complexity to the Web server setup. Both the host OS and guest OS need to be secured. If the virtualization technology supports it, a copy of each guest OS and installed Web server application should be backed up to allow restoration if an attack or other disruption occurs. The Web server and its guest OS, the host OS, and the virtualization software should all be patched in a timely manner. It is important to note that if the guest OS or applications become compromised, the guest virtual machine can infect other hosts on the network as if it were a standalone physical host. Each guest OS and associated Web server software should be configured and maintained following the recommendations in this publication.

3.7 Checklist for Planning and Managing Web Servers

Completed	Action
	Plan the configuration and deployment of the Web server
☐	Identify functions of the Web server
☐	Identify categories of information that will be stored, processed, and transmitted through the Web server
☐	Identify security requirements of information
☐	Identify how information is published to the Web server
☐	Identify the security requirements of other hosts involved (e.g., backend database or Web service)
☐	Identify a dedicated host to run the Web server
☐	Identify network services that will be provided or supported by the Web server
☐	Identify the security requirements of any additional services provided or supported by the Web server
☐	Identify how the Web server will be managed
☐	Identify users and categories of users of the Web server and determine privilege for each category of user
☐	Identify user authentication methods for the Web server and how authentication data will be protected
☐	Identify how access to information resources will be enforced

Completed	Action
☐	Identify appropriate physical security mechanisms
☐	Identify appropriate availability mechanisms
	Choose appropriate OS for Web server
☐	Minimal exposure to vulnerabilities
☐	Ability to restrict administrative or root level activities to authorized users only
☐	Ability to control access to data on the server
☐	Ability to disable unnecessary network services that may be built into the OS or server software
☐	Ability to control access to various forms of executable programs, such as CGI scripts and server plug-ins
☐	Ability to log appropriate server activities to detect intrusions and attempted intrusions
☐	Provision of a host-based firewall capability
☐	Availability of experienced staff to install, configure, secure, and maintain OS
	Choose appropriate platform for Web server
☐	General purpose OS Trusted OS Web server appliance Pre-hardened OS and Web server Virtualized platform

4. Securing the Web Server Operating System

Protecting a Web server from compromise involves hardening the underlying OS, the Web server application, and the network to prevent malicious entities from directly attacking the Web server. The first step in securing a Web server, hardening the underlying OS, is discussed at length in this section. (Securing the Web server application and the network are addressed in Sections 5 and 8, respectively.)

All commonly available Web servers operate on a general-purpose OS. Many security issues can be avoided if the OSs underlying the Web servers are configured appropriately. Default hardware and software configurations are typically set by manufacturers to emphasize features, functions, and ease of use, at the expense of security. Because manufacturers are unaware of each organization's security needs, each Web server administrator must configure new servers to reflect their organization's security requirements and reconfigure them as those requirements change. The practices recommended here are designed to help Web server administrators configure and deploy Web servers that satisfy their organizations' security requirements. Web server administrators managing existing Web servers should confirm that their systems address the issues discussed.

The techniques for hardening different OSs vary greatly; therefore, this section includes the generic procedures common in securing most OSs. Security configuration guides and checklists for many OSs are publicly available; these documents typically contain recommendations for settings that improve the default level of security, and they may also contain step-by-step instructions for securing systems.[16] In addition, many organizations maintain their own guidelines specific to their requirements. Some automated tools also exist for hardening OSs, and their use is strongly recommended (see Appendix D).

Five basic steps are necessary to maintain basic OS security:

■ Planning the installation and deployment of the host OS and other components for the Web server

■ Patching and updating the host OS as required

■ Hardening and configuring the host OS to address security adequately

■ Installing and configuring additional security controls, if needed

■ Testing the host OS to ensure that the previous four steps adequately addressed all security issues.

The first step is discussed in Section 3. The other steps are covered in Sections 4.1 and 4.2.

4.1 Installing and Configuring the Operating System

This section provides an overview of the second, third, and fourth steps in the list above. The combined result of these steps should be a reasonable level of protection for the Web server's OS.

4.1.1 Patch and Upgrade Operating System

Once an OS is installed, applying needed patches or upgrades to correct for known vulnerabilities is essential. Any known vulnerabilities an OS has should be corrected before using it to host a Web server

---

[16] Checklists and implementation guides for various operating systems and applications are available from NIST at http://checklists.nist.gov/. Also, see NIST SP 800-70, *Security Configuration Checklists Program for IT Products*, available at the same Web site, for general information about NIST's checklists program.

or otherwise exposing it to untrusted users. To adequately detect and correct these vulnerabilities, Web server administrators should do the following:

■ Create, document, and implement a patching process.[17]

■ Identify vulnerabilities and applicable patches.[18]

■ Mitigate vulnerabilities temporarily if needed and if feasible (until patches are available, tested, and installed).

■ Install permanent fixes (commonly called patches, hotfixes, service packs, or updates).

Administrators should ensure that Web servers, particularly new ones, are adequately protected during the patching process. For example, a Web server that is not fully patched or not configured securely could be compromised by threats if it is publicly accessible while it is being patched. When preparing new Web servers for deployment, administrators should do either of the following:

■ Keep the servers disconnected from networks or connect them only to an isolated "build" network until all patches have been transferred to the servers through out-of-band means (e.g., CDs) and installed, and the other configuration steps listed in Section 4.1 have been performed.

■ Place the servers on a virtual local area network (VLAN)[19] or other network segment that severely restricts what actions the hosts on it can perform and what communications can reach the hosts—only allowing those events that are necessary for patching and configuring the hosts. Do not transfer the hosts to regular network segments until all the configuration steps listed in Section 4.1 have been performed.

Administrators should generally not apply patches to Web servers without first testing them on another identically configured system because patches can inadvertently cause unexpected problems with proper system operation. Although administrators can configure Web servers to download patches automatically, the servers should not be configured to install them automatically so that they can first be tested.

4.1.2 Remove or Disable Unnecessary Services and Applications

Ideally, a Web server should be on a dedicated, single-purpose host. When configuring the OS, disable everything except that which is expressly permitted—that is, disable all services and applications, re-enable only those required by the Web server, and then remove the unneeded services and applications. If possible, install the minimal OS configuration and then add or remove services and applications as needed. Choose the "minimal installation" option, if available, to minimize the effort required in removing unnecessary services. Furthermore, many uninstall scripts or programs are far from perfect in completely removing all components of a service; therefore, it is always better not to install unnecessary

---

[17] For more information, see NIST SP 800-40 Version 2.0, *Creating a Patch and Vulnerability Management Program*, which is available at http://csrc.nist.gov/publications/nistpubs/. A single patch management process can be put into place for both operating systems and applications (including Web server software).

[18] To check for vulnerabilities in OSs, services, and other applications, see the NIST National Vulnerability Database (NVD) at http://nvd.nist.gov/.

[19] VLANs can easily be misconfigured in ways that reduce or eliminate their effectiveness as a security control. Organizations planning to use VLANs should ensure that they are configured properly and that any configuration changes are carefully verified.

services. Some common types of services and applications that should usually be disabled if not required include the following:

- File and printer sharing services (e.g., Windows Network Basic Input/Output System [NetBIOS] file and printer sharing, Network File System [NFS], File Transfer Protocol [FTP])

- Wireless networking services

- Remote control and remote access programs, particularly those that do not strongly encrypt their communications (e.g., Telnet)[20]

- Directory services (e.g., Lightweight Directory Access Protocol [LDAP], Kerberos, Network Information System [NIS])

- Email services (e.g., Simple Mail Transfer Protocol [SMTP])

- Language compilers and libraries

- System development tools

- System and network management tools and utilities, including Simple Network Management Protocol (SNMP).

Removing unnecessary services and applications is preferable to simply disabling them through configuration settings because attacks that attempt to alter settings and activate a disabled service cannot succeed when the functional components are completely removed. Disabled services could also be enabled inadvertently through human error.

Eliminating or disabling unnecessary services enhances the security of a Web server in several ways [Alle00]:

- Other services cannot be compromised and used to attack the host or impair the services of the Web server. Each service added to a host increases the risk of compromise for that host because each service is another possible avenue of access for an attacker. Less is more secure in this case.

- Other services may have defects or may be incompatible with the Web server itself. By disabling or removing them, they should not affect the Web server and should potentially improve its availability.

- The host can be configured to better suit the requirements of the particular service. Different services might require different hardware and software configurations, which could lead to unnecessary vulnerabilities or negatively affect performance.

- By reducing services, the number of logs and log entries is reduced; therefore, detecting unexpected behavior becomes easier (see Section 9).

Organizations should determine the services to be enabled on a Web server. Services in addition to the Web server service that might be installed include database access protocols, file transfer protocols, and

---

[20] If a remote control or remote access program is absolutely required and it does not strongly encrypt its communications, it should be tunneled over a protocol that provides encryption, such as secure shell (SSH) or IP Security (IPsec). Section 7 provides additional information on requirements for cryptography.

remote administration services. These services may be required in certain instances, but they may increase the risks to the server. Whether the risks outweigh the benefits is a decision for each organization to make.

4.1.3 Configure Operating System User Authentication

For Web servers, the authorized users who can configure the OS are limited to a small number of designated Web server administrators and Webmasters. The users who can access the public Web server, however, may range from unrestricted to restricted subsets of the Internet community. To enforce policy restrictions, if required, the Web server administrator should configure the OS to authenticate a prospective user by requiring proof that the user is authorized for such access. Even though a Web server may allow unauthenticated access to most of its services, administrative and other types of specialized access should be limited to specific individuals and groups.

Enabling authentication by the host computer involves configuring parts of the OS, firmware, and applications on the server, such as the software that implements a network service. Although not normally the case for public Web servers, in special situations, such as high-value/high-risk sites, organizations may also use authentication hardware, such as tokens or one-time password devices. Use of authentication mechanisms where authentication information is reusable (e.g., passwords) and transmitted in the clear over a network is strongly discouraged because the information can be intercepted and used by an attacker to masquerade as an authorized user.

To ensure the appropriate user authentication is in place, take the following steps [Alle00]:

■ **Remove or Disable Unneeded Default Accounts and Groups**—The default configuration of the OS often includes guest accounts (with and without passwords), administrator or root level accounts, and accounts associated with local and network services. The names and passwords for those accounts are well known. Remove or disable unnecessary accounts to eliminate their use by attackers, including guest accounts on computers containing sensitive information. If there is no requirement to retain a guest account or group, severely restrict access to it and change the password in accordance with the organizational password policy.

For default accounts that need to be retained, change the names (where possible and particularly for administrator or root level accounts) and passwords to be consistent with the organizational password policy. Default account names and passwords are commonly known in the attacker community.

■ **Disable Non-Interactive Accounts**—Disable accounts (and the associated passwords) that need to exist but do not require an interactive login. For Unix systems, disable the login shell or provide a login shell with NULL functionality (e.g., /bin/false).

■ **Create the User Groups**—Assign users to the appropriate groups. Then assign rights to the groups, as documented in the deployment plan. This approach is preferable to assigning rights to individual users, which becomes unwieldy with large numbers of users.

■ **Create the User Accounts**—The deployment plan identifies who will be authorized to use each computer and its services. Create only the necessary accounts. Permit the use of shared accounts only when no viable alternatives exist.

■ **Check the Organization's Password Policy**—Set account passwords appropriately. This policy should address the following:

- **Length**—a minimum length for passwords. Specify a minimum length of at least eight characters.

- **Complexity**—the mix of characters required. Require passwords to contain both uppercase and lowercase letters and at least one nonalphabetic character, and to not be a "dictionary" word.

- **Aging**—how long a password may remain unchanged. Require users to change their passwords periodically. Administrator or root level passwords should be changed every 30 to 120 days. The period for user-level passwords should be determined by the enforced length and complexity of the password combined with the sensitivity of the information protected. When considering the appropriate aging duration, the exposure level of user passwords should also be taken into account. Consideration should also be given to enforcing a minimum aging duration to prevent users from rapidly cycling through password changes to clear out their password history and bypass reuse restrictions.

- **Reuse**—whether a password may be reused. Some users try to defeat a password aging requirement by changing the password to one they have used previously. If possible, ensure that users cannot change their passwords by merely appending characters to the beginning or end of their original passwords (e.g., original password was "mysecret" and is changed to "1mysecret" or "mysecret1").

- **Authority**—who is allowed to change or reset passwords and what sort of proof is required before initiating any changes.

- **Password Security**—how passwords should be secured, such as not storing passwords unencrypted on the mail server, and requiring administrators to use different passwords for their email administration accounts than their other administration accounts.

■ **Configure Computers to Prevent Password Guessing**—It is relatively easy for an unauthorized user to try to gain access to a computer by using automated software tools that attempt all passwords. If the OS provides the capability, configure it to increase the period between login attempts with each unsuccessful attempt. If that is not possible, the alternative is to deny login after a limited number of failed attempts (e.g., three). Typically, the account is "locked out" for a period of time (such as 30 minutes) or until a user with appropriate authority reactivates it.

The choice to deny login is another situation that requires the Web server administrator to make a decision that balances security and convenience. Implementing this recommendation can help prevent some kinds of attacks, but it can also allow an attacker to use failed login attempts to prevent user access, resulting in a DoS condition. The risk of DoS from account lockout is much greater if an attacker knows or can surmise a pattern to your naming convention that allows them to guess account names.

Failed network login attempts should not prevent an authorized user or administrator from logging in at the console. Note that all failed login attempts, whether via the network or console, should be logged. If remote administration is not to be implemented (see Section 9.5), disable the ability for the administrator or root level accounts to log in from the network.

■ **Install and Configure Other Security Mechanisms to Strengthen Authentication**—If the information on the Web server requires it, consider using other authentication mechanisms such as biometrics, smart cards, client/server certificates, or one-time password systems. They can be more expensive and difficult to implement, but they may be justified in some circumstances. When such authentication mechanisms and devices are used, the organization's policy should be changed accordingly, if necessary. Some organizational policies may already require the use of strong authentication mechanisms.

As mentioned earlier, attackers using network sniffers can easily capture passwords passed across a network in clear text. However, passwords are economical and appropriate if properly protected while in transit. Organizations should implement authentication and encryption technologies, such as Secure Sockets Layer (SSL)/Transport Layer Security (TLS), Secure Shell (SSH), or virtual private networking (VPN), to protect passwords during transmission. Requiring user-friendly server authentication to be used with encryption technologies reduces the likelihood of successful man-in-the-middle and spoofing attacks.

4.1.4 Configure Resource Controls Appropriately

All commonly used modern server OSs provide the capability to specify access privileges individually for files, directories, devices, and other computational resources. By carefully setting access controls and denying personnel unauthorized access, the Web server administrator can reduce intentional and unintentional security breaches. For example, denying read access to files and directories helps to protect confidentiality of information, and denying unnecessary write (modify) access can help maintain the integrity of information. Limiting the execution privilege of most system-related tools to authorized system administrators can prevent users from making configuration changes that could reduce security. It also can restrict the attacker's ability to use those tools to attack the system or other systems on the network.

4.1.5 Install and Configure Additional Security Controls

OSs often do not include all of the security controls necessary to secure the OS, services, and applications adequately. In such cases, administrators need to select, install, and configure additional software to provide the missing controls. Commonly needed controls include the following:

■ Anti-malware software, such as antivirus software, anti-spyware software, and rootkit detectors, to protect the local OS from malware and to detect and eradicate any infections that occur.[21] Examples of when anti-malware software would be helpful include a Web administrator bringing infected media to the Web server and a network service worm contacting the server and infecting it.

■ Host-based intrusion detection and prevention software, to detect attacks performed against the Web server, including DoS attacks. Section 7.2.2 contains additional information on host-based intrusion detection and prevention software.

■ Host-based firewalls, to protect the server from unauthorized access.[22]

■ Patch management software to ensure that vulnerabilities are addressed promptly. Patch management software can be used only to apply patches or also to identify new vulnerabilities in the Web server's OSs, services, and applications.

---

[21]   Additional information on anti-malware software is available from NIST SP 800-83, *Guide to Malware Incident Prevention and Handling* (http://csrc.nist.gov/publications/nistpubs/).

[22]   For more information on firewalls, see NIST SP 800-41, *Guidelines on Firewalls and Firewall Policy* (http://csrc.nist.gov/publications/nistpubs/).

Some Web server administrators also install one or more forms of host-based intrusion detection or intrusion prevention software on their servers. For example, file integrity checking software can identify changes to critical system files.

When planning security controls, Web server administrators should consider the resources that the security controls will consume. A server's performance could degrade if it does not have enough memory and processing capacity for the controls.

4.2 Security Testing the Operating System

Periodic security testing of the OS is a vital way to identify vulnerabilities and to ensure that the existing security precautions are effective. Common methods for testing OSs include vulnerability scanning and penetration testing. Vulnerability scanning usually entails using an automated vulnerability scanner to scan a host or group of hosts on a network for application, network, and OS vulnerabilities. Penetration testing is a testing process designed to compromise a network using the tools and methodologies of an attacker. It involves iteratively identifying and exploiting the weakest areas of the network to gain access to the remainder of the network, eventually compromising the overall security of the network. Vulnerability scanning should be conducted periodically, at least weekly to monthly, and penetration testing should be conducted at least annually. Because both of these testing techniques are also applicable to testing the Web server application, they are discussed in detail in Section 9.4.[23]

Testing generally should not be performed on the production Web server itself. As mentioned in Section 4.1.1, testing for patches and changes to the system should be performed on a separate system; this same testing environment should be used to perform security testing of the Web server.

4.3 Checklist for Securing the Web Server Operating System

Completed	Action
	Patch and upgrade OS
☐	Create, document, and implement a patching process
☐	Keep the servers disconnected from networks or on an isolated network that severely restricts communications until all patches have been installed
☐	Identify and install all necessary patches and upgrades to the OS
☐	Identify and install all necessary patches and upgrades to applications and services included with the OS
☐	Identify and mitigate any unpatched vulnerabilities
	Remove or disable unnecessary services and applications
☐	Disable or remove unnecessary services and applications
	Configure OS user authentication
☐	Remove or disable unneeded default accounts and groups
☐	Disable non-interactive accounts
☐	Create the user groups for the particular computer
☐	Create the user accounts for the particular computer
☐	Check the organization's password policy and set account passwords appropriately (e.g., length, complexity)

---

[23] For information on other testing techniques, see NIST SP 800-42, *Guideline on Network Security Testing* (http://csrc.nist.gov/publications/nistpubs/).

Completed	Action
☐	Prevent password guessing (e.g., increase the period between attempts, deny login after a defined number of failed attempts)
☐	Install and configure other security mechanisms to strengthen authentication
	Configure resource controls appropriately
☐	Deny read access to unnecessary files and directories
☐	Deny write access to unnecessary files and directories
☐	Limit the execution privilege of system tools to system administrators
	Install and configure additional security controls
☐	Select, install, and configure additional software to provide needed controls not included in the OS, such as antivirus software, antispyware software, rootkit detectors, host-based intrusion detection and prevention software, host-based firewalls, and patch management software
	Test the security of the OS
☐	Identify a separate identical system
☐	Test OS after initial install to determine vulnerabilities
☐	Test OS periodically (e.g., quarterly) to determine new vulnerabilities

5. Securing the Web Server

Once the OS has been installed and secured, installing the chosen Web server software can begin. Before starting this process, read the Web server manufacturer's documentation carefully and understand the various options available during the installation process. Also, be sure to visit the manufacturer's Web site or a vulnerability database Web site, such as the National Vulnerability Database (NVD),[24] to determine whether there are known vulnerabilities and related patches available that should be installed or configured as part of the setup process. Only after these preliminary steps are accomplished should the installation be started. Note that this section discusses only generic installation and configuration procedures; specific directions for particular Web servers are available from Web server manufacturers and from security checklist repositories.[25]

A partially configured and/or patched server should not be exposed to external networks (e.g., the Internet) or external users. In addition, internal network access should be as limited as possible until all software is installed, patched, and configured securely. Insecure Web servers can be compromised in a matter of minutes after being placed on the Internet. While it is ideal to fully harden the platform before placing it on the network, it is not always feasible. For example, some application development tool combinations cannot be installed, configured, and tested on top of a pre-hardened OS and Web server configuration. In such situations, stepwise or incremental hardening is a viable option to consider, with full validation of complete hardening occurring at production deployment.

5.1 Securely Installing the Web Server

In many respects, the secure installation and configuration of the Web server application mirrors the OS process discussed in Section 4. The overarching principle, as before, is to install only the services required for the Web server and to eliminate any known vulnerabilities through patches or upgrades. Any unnecessary applications, services, or scripts that are installed should be removed immediately once the installation process is complete. During the installation of the Web server, the following steps should be performed:

■ Install the Web server software either on a dedicated host or on a dedicated guest OS if virtualization is being employed.

■ Apply any patches or upgrades to correct for known vulnerabilities.

■ Create a dedicated physical disk or logical partition (separate from OS and Web server application) for Web content.

■ Remove or disable all services installed by the Web server application but not required (e.g., gopher, FTP, remote administration).

■ Remove or disable all unneeded default login accounts created by the Web server installation.

■ Remove all manufacturers' documentation from the server.

■ Remove all example or test files from the server, including scripts and executable code.

---

[24] NVD is available at http://nvd.nist.gov/.
[25] NIST hosts a security checklist repository at http://checklists.nist.gov/.

■ Apply appropriate security template or hardening script to server.

■ Reconfigure HTTP service banner (and others as required) not to report Web server and OS type and version (this may not be possible with all Web servers).

Organizations should consider installing the Web server with non-standard directory names, directory locations, and filenames. Many Web server attack tools and worms targeting Web servers only look for files and directories in their default locations. While this will not stop determined attackers, it will force them to work harder to compromise the server, and it also increases the likelihood of attack detection because of the failed attempts to access the default filenames and directories and the additional time needed to perform an attack.

5.2   Configuring Access Controls

Most Web server host OSs provide the capability to specify access privileges individually for files, devices, and other computational resources on that host. Any information that the Web server can access using these controls can potentially be distributed to all users accessing the public Web site. The Web server software is likely to include mechanisms to provide additional file, device, and resource access controls specific to its operation. It is important to set identical permissions for both the OS and Web server application; otherwise, too much or too little access may be granted to users. Web server administrators should consider how best to configure access controls to protect information stored on public Web servers from two perspectives:

■ Limit the access of the Web server application to a subset of computational resources.

■ Limit the access of users through additional access controls enforced by the Web server, where more detailed levels of access control are required.

The proper setting of access controls can help prevent the disclosure of sensitive or restricted information that is not intended for public dissemination. In addition, access controls can be used to limit resource use in the event of a DoS attack against the Web server. Similarly, access controls can enforce separation of duty by ensuring Web server logs cannot be modified by Web server administrators and potentially ensure that the Web server process is only allowed to append to the log files.

Typical files to which access should be controlled are as follows:

■ Application software and configuration files

■ Files related directly to security mechanisms:

  ■ Password hash files and other files used in authentication

  ■ Files containing authorization information used in controlling access

  ■ Cryptographic key material used in confidentiality, integrity, and non-repudiation services

■ Server log and system audit files

■ System software and configuration files

■ Web content files.

5.2.1   Configuring the Permissions of the Web Server Application

It is vital that the Web server application executes only under a unique individual user and group identity with very restrictive access controls.[26] New user and group identities should be established for exclusive use by the Web server software. The new user and new group should be independent from all other users and groups and unique. This is a prerequisite for implementing the access controls described in the following steps. During initialization, the server may have to run with root (Unix) or administrator/system (Windows) privileges to bind to Transmission Control Protocol (TCP) ports numbered below 1024 (80 and 443 are the default ports for HTTP and HTTPS). Ensure that the Web server is configured to reduce its privileges to those of the Web server user after performing its initialization functions.

In addition, use the Web server OS to limit which files can be accessed by the Web server's service processes. These processes should have read-only access to those files necessary to perform the service and should have no access to other files, such as server log files. Use Web server host OS access controls to enforce the following [Koss00]:

- Service processes are configured to run as a user with a strictly limited set of privileges (i.e., not running as root, administrator, or equivalent).

- Web content files can be read but not written by service processes.

- Service processes cannot write to the directories where public Web content is stored.

- Only processes authorized for Web server administration can write Web content files.

- The Web server application can write Web server log files, but log files cannot be read by the Web server application. Only root/system/administrative level processes can read Web server log files.

- Temporary files created by the Web server application, such as those that might be generated in the creation of dynamic Web pages or by users uploading content, are restricted to a specified and appropriately protected subdirectory (if possible).

- Access to any temporary files created by the Web server application is limited to the Web server processes that created the files (if possible).

It is also necessary to ensure that the Web server application cannot save (or, in some cases, read) files outside the specified file structure dedicated to public Web content. This may be a configuration choice in the server software, or it may be a choice in how the server process is controlled by the OS. Ensure that such directories and files (outside the specified directory tree) cannot be accessed, even if users perform direct browsing by accessing the URLs of those files or through directory traversal attacks against the Web server process.

To mitigate the effects of certain types of DoS attacks, configure the Web server to limit the amount of OS resources it can consume. Some examples include—

---

[26] On Unix systems, a Web server is typically assigned to its own unique group. On Windows, specific group settings may depend on the Web server installed. For example, the Apache 2.0 user in Windows should be a member of the Users group. More information is available at http://httpd.apache.org/docs/2.0/platform/windows.html.

■ Installing Web content on a different hard drive or logical partition than the OS and Web server application.

■ Placing a limit on the amount of hard drive space that is dedicated for uploads, if uploads to the Web server are allowed. Ideally, uploads should be placed on a separate partition to provide stronger assurance that the hard drive limit cannot be exceeded.

■ If uploads are allowed to the Web server, ensuring that these files are not readable by the Web server until after some automated or manual review process is used to screen them. This measure prevents the Web server from being used to propagate malware or traffic pirated software, attack tools, pornography, etc. It is also possible to limit the size of each uploaded file, which could limit the potential effects of a DoS attack involving uploading many large files.

■ Ensuring that log files are stored in a location that is sized appropriately. Ideally, log files should be stored on a separate partition. If an attack causes the size of the log files to increase beyond acceptable limits, a physical partition helps ensure the Web server has enough resources to handle the situation appropriately.

■ Configuring the maximum number of Web server processes and/or network connections that the Web server should allow.

To some degree, these actions protect against attacks that attempt to fill the file system on the Web server host OS with extraneous and incorrect information that may cause the system to crash. Logging information generated by the Web server host OS may help in recognizing such attacks. As discussed in Section 9.1, administrators should store Web server logs on centralized logging servers whenever possible and also store logs locally if feasible. If an attack causes the Web server to be compromised, the attacker could modify or erase locally stored logs to conceal information on the attack. Maintaining a copy of the logs on a centralized logging server gives administrators more information to use when investigating such a compromise.

In addition to the controls mentioned above, it is often necessary to configure timeouts and other controls to further reduce the impact of certain DoS attacks. One type of DoS attack takes advantage of the practical limits on simultaneous network connections by quickly establishing connections up to the maximum permitted, such that no new legitimate users can gain access. By setting network connection timeouts (the time after which an inactive connection is dropped) to a minimum acceptable time limit, established connections will time out as quickly as possible, opening up new connections to legitimate users. This measure only mitigates the effects; it does not defeat the attack.

If the maximum number of open connections (or connections that are half-open—that is, the first part of the TCP handshake was successful) is set to a low number, an attacker can easily consume the available connections with illegitimate requests (often called a SYN flood). Setting the maximum to a much higher number may mitigate the effect of such an attack, but at the expense of consuming additional resources. Note that this is only an issue for Web servers that are not protected by a firewall that stops SYN flood attacks. Most enterprise-level firewalls protect Web servers from SYN floods by intercepting them before they reach the Web servers.

5.2.2 Configuring Secure Web Content Directory

Do not use links, aliases, or shortcuts in the public Web content file directory tree that point to directories or files elsewhere on the server host or the network file system. If possible, disable the ability of the Web server software to follow links and aliases. As stated earlier, Web server log files and configuration files should reside outside the specified file directory tree for public Web content.

The following steps are required to restrict access to a specific Web content file directory tree:

■ Dedicate a single hard drive or logical partition for Web content and establish related subdirectories exclusively for Web server content files, including graphics but excluding scripts and other programs.

■ Define a single directory tree exclusively for all external scripts or programs executed as part of Web content (e.g., CGI, Active Server Page [ASP], PHP).

■ Disable the execution of scripts that are not exclusively under the control of administrative accounts. This action is accomplished by creating and controlling access to a separate directory intended to contain authorized scripts.

■ Disable the use of hard or symbolic links.

■ Define a complete Web content access matrix. Identify which folders and files within the Web server document should be restricted and which should be accessible (and by whom).

Most Web server software vendors provide directives or commands that allow the Web administrator to restrict user access to public Web server content files. For example, the Apache Web server software provides a <Limit> directive, which allows the Web administrator to restrict which optional access features (such as New, Delete, Connect, Head, and Get) are associated with each Web content file; any HTTP method omitted from the <Limit> directive will be allowed. Within the <Limit> directive, administrators can specify the requirements that must be met for the Limited action to be allowed. The Apache Require directive allows the Web administrator to restrict available content to authenticated users or groups.

Many directives or commands can be overridden on a per-directory basis. The convenience of being able to make local exceptions to global policy is offset by the threat of a security hole being introduced in a distant subdirectory, which could be controlled by a hostile user. The Web administrator should disable a subdirectory's ability to override top-level security directives unless that override is absolutely necessary.

In most cases, Web server file directory listings should be disabled. The HTTP specifies that a URL ending in a slash character be treated as a request for a listing of the files in the directory with that name. Web servers should be prohibited from responding to such requests with a file listing, even if the public can read all of the directory files. Such requests often indicate an attempt to locate information by means other than those intended by the Web administrator or Webmaster. Users may attempt this if they are having difficulty navigating through the site or if a link appears to be broken. Intruders may attempt this to locate information hidden by the Web site's interface. Web administrators should investigate requests of this type found in the Web server log files (see Section 9).

5.2.3 Uniform Resource Identifiers and Cookies

Uniform Resource Identifiers (URI) are the address technology from which URLs are created. Technically URLs (e.g., http://www.mywww.gov) are a subset of URIs. There are a number of security issues that arise from URIs. Because URIs are sent in the clear, any data stored within them can be easily compromised. For example, URIs are recorded in numerous locations, including Web browser logs (i.e., browser history), proxy server logs, and third-party HTTP referrer logs. Thus, hiding sensitive data such as usernames and passwords or hidden server resources in URIs is not recommended. Security through obscurity is not secure.

URIs are often included with public Web content. Although these URIs may not display as Web content in a user's Web browser, they can be easily discovered in the source code. Therefore, no publicly served Web content should include sensitive URIs hidden in the source code. Many attackers and malicious bots (see Section 5.2.4) search the source code for sensitive URI information, including—

■ E-mail addresses

■ Images on other servers

■ Links to other servers

■ Particular text expressions (e.g., userid, password, root, administrator)

■ Hidden form values

■ Hyperlinks.

A cookie is a small piece of information that may be written to the user's hard drive when the user visits a Web site. The intent of cookies is to allow servers to recognize a specific browser (user). In essence, they add state to the stateless HTTP protocol. Because cookies are usually sent in the clear and stored in the clear on the user's host, they are vulnerable to compromise. There are known vulnerabilities in certain versions of Internet Explorer, for example, that allow a malicious Web site to remotely collect all of a visitor's cookies without the visitor's knowledge. Therefore, cookies should never contain data that can be used directly by an attacker (e.g., username, password). OMB M-00-13[27] explicitly states that Federal Web sites should not use cookies unless there is a compelling need to gather the data on the site, and only with the appropriate approvals, notifications, and safeguards in place. For Web sites that need to maintain session information, the session identifier can be passed as part of the URL to the Web site rather than stored as a cookie. Regardless of whether cookies are being used or not, SSL/TLS should be used to prevent attackers from retrieving information from the HTTP messages sent over the network and using it to hijack a user's session.

5.2.4 Controlling Impact of Web "Bots" on Web Servers

Web bots (also known as crawlers or spiders) are software applications used to collect, analyze, and index Web content. Web bots are used by numerous organizations for many purposes. Some examples include—

■ MSNBot, Slurp, and Googlebot slowly and carefully analyze, index, and record Web sites for Web search engines such as Windows Live Search, Yahoo! and Google.

■ Mediabot is used by Google to analyze content served by an AdSense page so that contextually relevant ads will be supplied.

■ Hyperlink "validators" are used by Webmasters to automatically validate the hyperlinks on their Web site.

---

[27] OMB M-00-13, Office of Management and Budget Memorandum 2000-13, 2000, is available at http://www.whitehouse.gov/omb/memoranda/m00-13.html.

■ EmailSiphon and Cherry Picker are bots specifically designed to crawl Web sites for electronic mail (e-mail) addresses to add to spam mailing lists. These are common examples of bots that may have a negative impact on a Web site or its users.

■ Many spambots crawl Web sites for login forms to create free e-mail addresses from which to send spam or to spam blogs, guestbooks, wikis, and forums to boost the search engine rankings of a particular Web site.

■ Screen scrapers retrieve content from Web sites to put up a copy on another server. These copies can be used for phishing or for attempting to generate ad revenue by having users visit the copy.

■ Some malicious bots crawl Web sites looking for vulnerable applications containing sensitive data (e.g., Social Security Numbers [SSN], credit card data).

Bots can present a challenge to Webmasters' administration of their servers because—

■ Web servers often contain directories that do not need to be indexed.

■ Organizations might not want part of their site appearing in search engines.

■ Web servers often contain temporary pages that should not be indexed.

■ Organizations operating the Web server are paying for bandwidth and want to exclude robots and spiders that do not benefit their goals.

■ Bots are not always well written or well intentioned and can hit a Web site with extremely rapid requests, causing a reduction in responsiveness or outright DoS for legitimate users.

■ Bots may uncover information that the Webmaster would prefer remained secret or at least unadvertised (e.g., e-mail addresses).

Fortunately, Web administrators or the Webmaster can influence the behavior of most bots on their Web site. A series of agreements called the Robots Exclusion Protocol (REP) has been created. Although REP is not an official Internet standard, it is supported by most well-written and well-intentioned bots, including those used by most major search engines.

Web administrators who wish to limit bots' actions on their Web server need to create a plain text file named "robots.txt." The file must always have this name, and it must reside in the Web server's root document directory. In addition, only one file is allowed per Web site. Note that the robots.txt file is a standard that is voluntarily supported by bot programmers, so malicious bots (such as EmailSiphon and Cherry Picker) often ignore this file.[28]

The robots.txt file is a simple text file that contains some keywords and file specifications. Each line of the file is either blank or consists of a single keyword and its related information. The keywords are used to tell robots which portions of a Web site are excluded.

---

[28] Other methods for controlling malicious bots exist; however, they are changing constantly as the malicious bot operators and Web administrators develop new methods of counteracting each other's techniques. Given the constantly changing nature of this area, discussion of these techniques is beyond the scope of this document. More information is available at http://www.onguardonline.gov/spam.html.

The following keywords are allowed:

■ **User-agent** is the name of the robot or spider. A Web administrator may also include more than one agent name if the same exclusion is to apply to each specified bot. The entry is not case-sensitive (in other words, "googlebot" is the same as "GOOGLEBOT" and "GoogleBot").

An asterisk ("*") indicates a "default" record, which applies if no other match is found. For example, if you specify "GoogleBot" only, then the "*" would apply to any other robot.

■ **Disallow** tells the bot(s) specified in the user-agent field which sections of the Web site are excluded. For example, /images informs the bot not to open or index any files in the images directory or any subdirectories. Thus, the directory "/images/special/" would not be indexed by the excluded bot(s).

Note that "/do" matches any directory beginning with "/do" (e.g. /do, /document, /docs, etc.), whereas "/do/" matches only the directory named "/do/". A Web administrator can also specify individual files for exclusion. For example, the Web administrator could specify "/mydata/help.html" to prevent only that one file from being accessed by the bots. A value of just "/" indicates that nothing on the Web site is allowed to be accessed by the specified bot(s).

At least one disallow per user-agent record must exist.

There are many ways to use the robots.txt file. Some simple examples are as follows:

■ To disallow all (compliant) bots from specific directories:

> **User-agent: ***
> **Disallow: /images/**
> **Disallow: /banners/**
> **Disallow: /Forms/**
> **Disallow: /Dictionary/**
> **Disallow: /_borders/**
> **Disallow: /_fpclass/**
> **Disallow: /_overlay/**
> **Disallow: /_private/**
> **Disallow: /_themes/**

■ To disallow all (compliant) bots from the entire Web site:

> **User-agent: ***
> **Disallow: /**

■ To disallow a specific bot (in this case the Googlebot) from examining a specific Web page:

> **User-agent: GoogleBot**
> **Disallow: tempindex.htm**

Note that the robots.txt file is available to everyone and does not provide access control mechanisms to the disallowed files. Thus, a Web administrator should not specify the names of sensitive files or folders because attackers often analyze robots.txt files to guide their initial investigations of Web sites. If files or directories must be excluded, it is better to use password-protected pages that cannot be accessed by bots.

Password protection is the only reliable way to exclude noncompliant bots or curious users. See Section 7 for more information on Web-based authentication methods.

Often, spambots ignore robots.txt and search for email addresses on the Web site and/or forms to which they can submit spam-related content. Spambots that merely scan the Web site typically do not affect its availability. Nevertheless, it may be beneficial to prevent them from harvesting e-mail addresses by performing address munging [Unsp06]—displaying e-mail addresses in an alternative human-readable format, such as listing name@mywww.gov as <name at mywww dot gov>. Unfortunately, these techniques do not stop all spambots. The best defense against address harvesting is not to display e-mail addresses.

Spambots searching for Web forms to submit spam-related content are a direct threat to the Web site. They can affect the organization's image if visitors view the submitted content as an endorsement. They may also affect the Web site's availability by making it difficult for users to find necessary content. There are several techniques available to reduce the amount of spam submissions, including—

- Blocking form submissions that use spam-related keywords

- Using the **rel="nofollow"** keyword in all submitted links, which will cause search engines to omit the links in their page-ranking algorithms, directly affecting the goals of a spambot [Google05]

- Requiring submitters to solve a Completely Automated Public Turing Test to Tell Computers and Humans Apart (CAPTCHA) prior to being allowed to submit content.

These techniques all have benefits and drawbacks associated with them. For example, some CAPTCHA techniques, which can be implemented as an obscured word in an image, do not comply with American Disability Association (ADA) or Section 508 accessibility guidelines. Information about ongoing research on detecting spambots can be found through the Adversarial Information Retrieval on the Web (AIRWeb) workshops.[29]

5.3 Checklist for Securing the Web Server

Completed	Action
	Securely install the Web server
☐	Install the Web server software on a dedicated host or a dedicated virtualized guest OS
☐	Apply any patches or upgrades to correct for known vulnerabilities
☐	Create a dedicated physical disk or logical partition (separate from OS and Web server application) for Web content
☐	Remove or disable all services installed by the Web server application but not required (e.g., gopher, FTP, remote administration)
☐	Remove or disable all unneeded default login accounts created by the Web server installation
☐	Remove all manufacturer documentation from server
☐	Remove any example or test files from server, including scripts and executable code
☐	Apply appropriate security template or hardening script to the server

---

[29] The AIRWeb 2006 Web site is available at http://airweb.cse.lehigh.edu/2006.

Completed	Action
☐	Reconfigure HTTP service banner (and others as required) NOT to report Web server and OS type and version
	Configure OS and Web server access controls
☐	Configure the Web server process to run as a user with a strictly limited set of privileges
☐	Configure the Web server so that Web content files can be read but not written by service processes
☐	Configure the Web server so that service processes cannot write to the directories where public Web content is stored
☐	Configure the Web server so that only processes authorized for Web server administration can write Web content files
☐	Configure the host OS so that the Web server can write log files but not read them
☐	Configure the host OS so that temporary files created by the Web server application are restricted to a specified and appropriately protected subdirectory
☐	Configure the host OS so that access to any temporary files created by the Web server application is limited to the service processes that created the files
☐	Install Web content on a different hard drive or logical partition than the OS and Web server application
☐	If uploads are allowed to the Web server, configure it so that a limit is placed on the amount of hard drive space that is dedicated for this purpose; uploads should be placed on a separate partition
☐	Ensure that log files are stored in a location that is sized appropriately; log files should be placed on a separate partition
☐	Configure the maximum number of Web server processes and/or network connections that the Web server should allow
☐	Ensure that any virtualized guest OSs follow this checklist
☐	Ensure users and administrators are able to change passwords
☐	Disable users after a specified period of inactivity
☐	Ensure each user and administrator has a unique ID
	Configure a secure Web content directory
☐	Dedicate a single hard drive or logical partition for Web content and establish related subdirectories exclusively for Web server content files, including graphics but excluding scripts and other programs
☐	Define a single directory exclusively for all external scripts or programs executed as part of Web server content (e.g., CGI, ASP)
☐	Disable the execution of scripts that are not exclusively under the control of administrative accounts. This action is accomplished by creating and controlling access to a separate directory intended to contain authorized scripts
☐	Disable the use of hard or symbolic links (e.g., shortcuts for Windows)
☐	Define a complete Web content access matrix. Identify which folders and files within the Web server document should be restricted and which should be accessible (and by whom)
☐	Check the organization's password policy and set account passwords appropriately (e.g., length, complexity)
☐	Use the robots.txt file, if appropriate
☐	Configure anti-spambot protection, if appropriate (e.g., CAPTCHAs, nofollow, or keyword filtering)

6. Securing Web Content

The two main components of Web security are the security of the underlying server application and OS, and the security of the actual content. Of these, the security of the content is often overlooked. Maintaining effective content security itself has two components. The more obvious is not placing any proprietary, classified, or other sensitive information on a publicly accessible Web server, unless other steps have been taken to protect the information via user authentication and encryption (see Section 7). The less obvious component of content security is avoiding compromises caused by the way particular types of content are processed on a server. As organizations have gotten better at protecting and hardening their network perimeters, OSs, and Web servers, attackers have increasingly turned to exploiting vulnerabilities in Web applications and the way information is processed on Web servers. These application layer attacks exploit the interactive elements of Web sites.

6.1   Publishing Information on Public Web Sites

Too often, little thought is given to the security implications of the content placed on the Web site. Many organizations do not have a Web publishing process or policy that determines what type of information to publish openly, what information to publish with restricted access, and what information should be omitted from any publicly accessible repository. This is troublesome because Web sites are often one of the first places that malicious entities search for valuable information. For example, attackers often read the contents of a target organization's Web site to gather intelligence before any attacks [Scam01]. Also, attackers can take advantage of content available on a Web site to craft a social engineering attack or to use individuals' identifying information in identity theft [FTC06].

Absent compelling reasons, a public Web site should not contain the following information:

■ Classified records

■ Internal personnel rules and procedures

■ Sensitive or proprietary information

■ Personal information about an organization's personnel or users[30]

    ■ Home addresses and telephone numbers

    ■ Uniquely identifying information, particularly SSNs

    ■ Detailed biographical material (that could be employed for social engineering)

    ■ Staff family members

■ Telephone numbers, e-mail addresses,[31] or general listings of staff unless necessary to fulfill organizational requirements

---

[30] For Federal agencies, this would include all items covered by the Privacy Act of 1974 (http://www.usdoj.gov/04foia/privstat.htm). This encompasses personally identifiable information (PII), which is information that can be used to uniquely identify, locate, or contact an individual.

[31] When an email address must be published on a Web site, consider the use of generic email addresses or aliases (e.g., webmaster@mydomain.gov as opposed to jane_doe@mydomain.gov). There are two reasons to do this. One, published

- Schedules of organizational principals or their exact location (whether on or off the premises)

- Information on the composition or preparation of hazardous materials or toxins[32]

- Sensitive information relating to homeland security

- Investigative records

- Financial records (beyond those already publicly available)

- Medical records

- The organization's physical and information security procedures

- Information about organization's network and information system infrastructure (e.g., address ranges, naming conventions, access numbers)

- Information that specifies or implies physical security vulnerabilities

- Plans, maps, diagrams, aerial photographs, and architectural plans of organizational building, properties, or installations

- Information on disaster recovery or continuity of operations plans except as absolutely required

- Details on emergency response procedures, evacuation routes, or organizational personnel responsible for these issues

- Copyrighted material without the written permission of the owner

- Privacy or security policies that indicate the types of security measures in place to the degree that they may be useful to an attacker.

Organizations should not use public Web servers to host sensitive information intended to be accessed only by internal users. The compromise of a public Web server often leads to the compromise of such data.

To ensure a consistent approach, an organization should create a formal policy and process for determining and approving the information to be published on a Web server. In many organizations, this is the responsibility of the CIO and/or public affairs officer. Such a process should include the following steps:

- Identify information that should be published on the Web

- Identify the target audience (Why publish if no audience exists?)

- Identify possible negative ramifications of publishing the information

---

email addresses are much more likely to receive spam. Two, personally identifying email addresses can provide useful information to an attacker (e.g., possible usernames, information for social engineering attempts).

[32] For more guidance on protecting this type of information, see the White House Memorandum dated March 19, 2000, *Action to Safeguard Information Regarding Weapons of Mass Destruction and Other Sensitive Documents Related to Homeland Security* (http://www.usdoj.gov/oip/foiapost/2002foiapost10.htm).

■ Identify who should be responsible for creating, publishing, and maintaining this particular information

■ Create or format information for Web publishing

■ Review the information for sensitivity and distribution/release controls (including the sensitivity of the information in aggregate)

■ Determine the appropriate access and security controls

■ Publish information

■ Verify published information

■ Periodically review published information to confirm continued compliance with organizational guidelines.

Any policy or process for determining and approving the information to be published on a Web server can benefit from the use of automated tools. Tools can scan incoming content for keywords, formatting, or metadata, and flag it for review, easing the burden of those required to verify content. Similarly, an internal automated system that allows users to post potential material to an internal Web site and notifies approving personnel (possibly via e-mail) of the posting allows material to be reviewed and posted to the public Web site more quickly through a repeatable process. Using an automated system also aids accountability because logs track who submitted the document and who approved it.

An often-overlooked area of Web content is the information sometimes hidden within the source code of a Web page. This information can be viewed from any Web browser using the "view source code" menu option. The source code can, for example, contain points of contact and reveal portions of the directory structure of the Web server. Organizations often do not pay attention to the contents of the source code on their Web sites, even though this code may contain sensitive information. Attackers scour not only the obvious content of the Web site but also details within the source code. Thus, Web administrators or Webmasters should periodically review code on their public Web server.

6.2   Observing Regulations about the Collection of Personal Information

Federal and state laws and regulations apply to the collection of user information on publicly accessible government Web sites. In addition, many government agencies have privacy guidelines that address the type of information that could be collected about users. Governmental organizations with Web sites should be aware of the appropriate and applicable laws, regulations, and agency guidelines. Private organizations may wish to use these guidelines and examples of sound security practices but should consult appropriate legal counsel and their privacy officials for the applicable legal and policy implications. However, Federal laws, regulations, and applicable agency guidelines do apply to commercial organizations that operate Web sites on behalf of Federal agencies. Organizations should be aware of changes to legal, regulatory, and contractual requirements and seek advice from knowledgeable legal and policy experts.

Federal agencies that collect PII must do so in accordance with Federal law and the Constitution. The Privacy Act, for example, requires agencies to minimize the information collected to that which is relevant and necessary to the business purpose,[33] and, in many cases, to collect information, to the greatest extent practicable, directly from the subject individual.[34] In addition, accepted practices (many of which are reflected in laws applicable to both private and public institutions) are to provide subject individuals:

■ Notice that information about them is being collected, including descriptions of what data is being collected, with whom it is being shared, and what is being done with that data

■ Opportunities to opt out of data collection unless the data collection is mandatory under law, necessary to the performance of a contract with the subject individual, or if the individual has freely offered his/her PII

■ Opportunities to access and review the records kept about themselves, and to request corrections or additions, especially if that information may be used to make a determination about the individuals' rights, opportunities, or benefits.

The following are examples of personal information:

■ Name

■ E-mail address

■ Mailing address

■ Telephone number

■ SSN

■ Financial information.

Federal agencies and many state agencies are also restricted in their ability to use Web browser cookies [OMB00a, OMB00b, OMB00c, and MASS99]. A cookie is a small piece of information that may be written to a user's hard drive when a Web site is visited. There are two principal types of cookies:

■ Persistent cookies cause the most concern. These cookies can be used to track activities of users over time and across different Web sites. The most common use of persistent cookies is to retain and correlate information about users between sessions. Federal agencies and many state agencies are generally prohibited from using persistent cookies on publicly accessible Web sites.

■ Session cookies are valid for a single session (visit) to a Web site. These cookies expire at the end of the session or within a limited time frame. Because these cookies cannot be used to track personal information, they are generally not subject to the prohibition that applies to persistent cookies. However, their use must be clearly stated and defined in the Web site's privacy statement.

---

[33] "Each agency that maintains a system of records shall....maintain in its records only such information about an individual as is relevant and necessary to accomplish a purpose of the agency required to be accomplished by statute or by Executive order of the President." Privacy Act, 5 USC § 552a(e)(1), http://www.usdoj.gov/oip/privstat.htm.

[34] "Each agency that maintains a system of records shall.... collect information to the greatest extent practicable directly from the subject individual when the information may result in adverse determinations about an individual's rights, benefits, and privileges under Federal programs." Privacy Act, 5 USC § 552a(e)(2), http://www.usdoj.gov/oip/privstat.htm.

6.3 Mitigating Indirect Attacks on Content

Indirect content attacks are not direct attacks on a Web server or its contents; they involve roundabout means to gain information from users who normally visit the Web site maintained on the Web server. The common theme of these attacks is to coerce users into visiting a malicious Web site set up by the attacker and divulging personal information in the belief that the site they visited is the legitimate Web site. While customers of electronic commerce and financial institutions are often targeted, such attacks are not limited to those Web sites. Besides acquiring personal information related to the targeted Web site, attacks may also be directed against the user's computer from the malicious Web site visited. The types of indirect attacks described in this section are phishing and pharming.

6.3.1 Phishing

Phishing attackers use social engineering techniques to trick users into accessing a fake Web site and divulging personal information. In some phishing attacks, attackers send a legitimate-looking e-mail asking users to update their information on the company's Web site, but the URLs in the e-mail actually point to a false Web site.[35] Other phishing attacks may be more advanced and take advantage of vulnerabilities in the legitimate Web site's application.[36]

Although phishing cannot be prevented entirely through technical means employed on a Web server, many techniques can reduce the likelihood that a Web site's users will be lured into a phishing attack[37] [Ollm04]:

■ Ensuring customer awareness of the dangers of phishing attacks and how to avoid them. The Federal Trade Commission (FTC) has posted a consumer alert outlining steps that users should take [FTC06a]:

  ▪ Do not reply to email messages or popup ads asking for personal or financial information.

  ▪ Do not trust telephone numbers in e-mails or popup ads. Voice over Internet Protocol technology can be used to register a telephone with any area code.

  ▪ Use antivirus, anti-spyware, and firewall software. These can detect malware on a user's machine that is participating in a phishing attack.

  ▪ Do not email personal or financial information.

  ▪ Review credit card and bank account statements regularly.

  ▪ Be cautious about accessing untrusted Web sites because some Web browser vulnerabilities can be exploited simply by visiting such sites. Users should also be cautious about opening any attachment or downloading any file from untrusted emails or Web sites.

  ▪ Forward phishing-related emails to spam@uce.gov and to the organization that is impersonated in the email.

---

[35] NIST SP 800-45 version 2, *Guidelines on Electronic Mail Security*, contains information on detecting phishing emails. It is available at http://csrc.nist.gov/publications/nistpubs/.

[36] An example of an advanced phishing attack occurred on the PayPal Web site [Netcraft06].

[37] Organizations should ensure that their internal users are also made aware of these techniques so that they can avoid phishing attacks directed at them.

- Request a copy of your credit report yearly from each of the three credit reporting agencies: Equifax, TransUnion, and Experian. If an identity thief opens accounts in your name, they will likely show up on your credit report.[38]

- Validating official communication by personalizing emails and providing unique identifying information that only the organization and user should know. However, confidential information should not be disclosed.

- Using digital signatures on e-mail. However, digital signatures may not be validated automatically by the user's email application.

- Performing content validation within the Web application. Vulnerabilities in the organization's Web applications may be used in a phishing attack.

- Personalizing Web content, which can aid users in identifying a fraudulent Web site.

- Using token-based or mutual authentication at the Web site to prevent phishers from reusing previous authentication information to impersonate the user.

Most Web browsers provide some level of phishing protection. All Web browsers inform users when they visit a secured site via a padlock or some other GUI mechanism, and they also inform users if the Domain Name System (DNS) address visited does not match that of the Public Key Infrastructure (PKI) certificate. However, phishing sites often use DNS addresses that are similar to those of the original sites and that have a valid PKI certificate, making them harder to detect. In such cases, a Web browser would notify the user of the danger only if the site was a known phishing site. Browsers may either download a phishing blacklist from the browser manufacturer's Web site periodically or check all Web requests against an anti-phishing database. Organizations should use Web browser-provided anti-phishing features where applicable. In addition, a number of vendors offer more advanced anti-phishing solutions and services [APWG07]:

- **Cousin Domain Monitoring and Prevention**—Vendors (primarily domain name registrars) monitor and in some instances prevent the creation of domain names similar to those of organizations that may be subject to phishing attacks.

- **Attack Detection and Analysis**—Vendors monitor e-mail and Web communication to discover ongoing phishing campaigns so that organizations can take appropriate responses.

- **Takedown**—Vendors aid in limiting access to the phishing Web site.

- **Fraud Analysis**—Vendors monitor access to the organization's Web site for potential fraud attempts (such as phishers attempting to use captured credentials) or monitor the Web for fraudulent use of an organization's identity.

- **Forensic Services**—After discovery of a successful phishing attack, vendors aid in addressing issues that arise as a result of the attack.

---

[38] Under the Fair and Accurate Credit Transactions Act of 2003, consumers can request a free credit report from each of the three consumer credit reporting companies once every 12 months. See http://www.ftc.gov/os/statutes/fcrajump.shtm for more information.

■ **Consumer Toolbars**—Vendors provide browser plug-ins that can provide or augment phishing detection available in users' browsers.

■ **E-mail Authentication**—Vendors provide secure e-mail solutions allowing users to discern whether or not an e-mail is from the organization itself or is a potential phishing attack.

■ **E-mail Filtering**—Vendors provide solutions to prevent an organization's internal users from receiving phishing e-mails.

■ **Web Filtering**—Vendors monitor an organization's outbound Web requests and prevent users from accessing known or suspected phishing Web sites.

■ **Authentication**—Vendors provide strong authentication solutions that are less susceptible to phishing attacks.

■ **Law Enforcement Enablement**—Vendors assist organizations in contacting law enforcement officials to aid in shutting down and prosecuting phishing attacks.

When contemplating anti-phishing measures, it is important to consider the type of information being hosted on the Web site. Web sites with little or no sensitive information may not need to implement more advanced or costly anti-phishing measures. Web sites storing PII should strongly consider implementing more robust anti-phishing measures.

6.3.2 Pharming

Pharming attackers use technical means, instead of social engineering, to redirect users into accessing a fake Web site masquerading as a legitimate one and divulging personal information. Pharming is normally accomplished either by exploiting vulnerabilities in DNS software, which is used to resolve human-readable Internet domain names into IP addresses, or by altering the host files maintained on a client computer for locally resolving Internet domain names. In either case, the affected system incorrectly resolves legitimate names to the malicious Web site address. Various techniques can help reduce the likelihood that a Web site's users become involved in a pharming attack [Ollm05]:

■ **Using the Current Versions of DNS Software with the Latest Security Patches Applied**—A compromised DNS server will allow attackers to direct users to a malicious server while maintaining a legitimate DNS name.

■ **Installing Server-Side DNS Protection Mechanisms Against Pharming**—There are tools available to mitigate threats to DNS software, such as the DNS Security Extensions; these are discussed in NIST SP 800-81, *Secure Domain Name System (DNS) Deployment Guide.*[39]

■ **Monitoring Organizational Domains and the Registration of Similar Domains**—Pharming attacks may take advantage of users who misspell the organization's domain name when accessing the site.

■ **Simplifying the Structure and Number of Organizational Domain Names**—If an organization has a complicated naming structure for its servers, it becomes increasingly difficult for users to discern whether they are on an illegitimate site. For example, many organizations will have users login at one

---

[39] NIST SP 800-81, *Secure Domain Name System (DNS) Deployment Guide*, is available at http://csrc.nist.gov/publications/nistpubs/

URL, such as https://www.organization.org/, but then redirect them to another URL, such as https://www.secure-organization.org/. A user redirected to https://www.secured-organization.org/ may not notice the attack.

■ **Using Secure Connections (i.e., HTTPS) for Logins, which Allows Users to Verify that the Server Certificates are Valid and Associated with a Legitimate Web Site**—Modern browsers will notify a user if the DNS name does not match the one provided by the certificate, but some pharming sites could have a legitimate certificate.[40]

■ **Ensuring User Awareness of the Dangers of Pharming Attacks and How to Avoid Them**— Pharming is a recent phenomenon; many users may not know to watch for pharming attacks.

■ **Verifying Third-Party Host Resolution**—A number of vendors provide third-party Web browser plug-ins[41] that support matching the Internet Protocol (IP) address of a Web site against a previously verified "good" IP address, providing users with a warning if the Web site is suspicious.

■ **Using Pre-Shared Secrets**—Pre-shared secrets can be used to prevent pharming attacks. A common implementation of pre-shared secrets is to have authorized users set up certain questions and answers that only they should know. In addition, the Web site provides each user with a specific image and/phrase that only it and the user knows. Subsequently, when a user logs in to the Web site, the user is asked one of the secret questions. If the user answers correctly, he or she is presented with the secret image/phrase and only then asked for a password. Since a pharming site would not know those pre-shared secrets and be able to respond accordingly, it should be recognizable as a malicious site. The main disadvantage of using pre-shared secrets is that user acceptance may be low because of the work involved to set up the secrets and log into a site. Moreover, some users might not recognize the missing data and use the pharming site anyway.

Many of the techniques used to prevent phishing attacks—particularly in commercial offerings—are relevant to preventing pharming attacks. As with anti-phishing solutions, when contemplating anti-pharming measures, it is important to consider the type of information being hosted on the Web site. Web sites with little or no sensitive information may not need to implement more advanced or costly anti-pharming measures. Web sites storing PII should strongly consider implementing more robust anti-pharming measures. Requiring strong authentication can greatly reduce the risk of successful phishing and pharming attacks.

6.4 Securing Active Content and Content Generation Technologies

In the early days of the Web, most sites presented textual, static HyperText Markup Language (HTML) pages. No interactivity occurred between the user and Web site beyond the user clicking on hyperlinks. Soon thereafter, various types of interactive elements were introduced that offered users new ways to

---

[40] In January 2001, VeriSign issued two Class 3 code-signing certificates to an individual claiming to be a Microsoft employee (http://www.microsoft.com/technet/security/bulletin/ms01-017.mspx). With TLS certificates available at less than $20 with little or no background check, it is becoming increasingly easier for attackers to acquire valid TLS certificates. While it is possible for Certificate Authorities (CA) to revoke certificates, most browsers are not configured to perform certificate revocation list checking. Section 7.5 provides more information about TLS.

[41] A plug-in is a program that works in conjunction with a Web browser to enhance the browser's capabilities. A browser typically prompts the user to download a new plug-in when content is encountered that requires functionality beyond the browser's existing capabilities.

interact more dynamically with Web sites. Unfortunately, these interactive elements introduced many Web-related vulnerabilities that remain a concern today.[42]

Active content refers to interactive program elements downloaded to the client (i.e., a Web browser) and processed there instead of the server. A variety of active content technologies exists; some of the more popular examples are ActiveX, Java, VBScript, JavaScript, and Asynchronous JavaScript and XML (AJAX). The use of active content often requires users to reduce the security settings on their Web browsers for processing to occur. If not implemented correctly, active content can present a serious threat to the end user. For example, active content can take actions independently without the knowledge or expressed consent of the user. While active content poses risk to the client, it can also pose risk to the Web server. The reason is that information processed on the client is under the control of the user, who can potentially manipulate the results by reverse engineering and tampering with the active content. For example, form validation processing done with active content elements on the client side can be changed to return out-of-range options or other unexpected results to the server. Therefore, the results of processing done on the client by elements of active content should not be trusted by the server; instead, the results should be verified by the server. Organizations considering the deployment of client-side active content should carefully consider the risks to both their users and their Web servers.

Content generators are programs on a Web server that dynamically generate HTML pages for users; these pages may be generated using information retrieved from a backend server, such as a database or directory, or possibly user-supplied input. Some of the earliest content generators were CGI scripts executed by the Web server when a specific URL was requested. In contrast, some modern content generators are an integral component of the servers on which they run, such as Java Enterprise Edition (Java EE) application servers. Because content generators are implemented on the server, they can open the Web server itself to threats. The danger with content generators occurs when they blindly accept input from users and apply it to actions taken on the Web server. If the content generator has not been implemented correctly to restrict input, an attacker can enter certain types of information that may negatively affect the Web server or compromise its security. For example, one common attack against content generators is Structured Query Language (SQL) injection. In this type of attack, a malicious entity sends specially crafted input to the content generator. The input includes a specific SQL command string that, when submitted unfiltered to a SQL database server, potentially returns to the attacker any or all of the information stored in the database. SQL injections and other attacks are used to execute commands or gain unauthorized access to the Web server or a backend database server.

All Web sites that implement active content and content generators should perform additional steps to protect the active content from compromise. These steps, which are discussed in the following sections, may not apply to all installations; therefore, they should be used as guidance in conjunction with appropriate manufacturer's documentation.

Special caution is also required for downloading preprogrammed scripts or executables from the Internet. Many Web administrators and Webmasters are tempted to save time by downloading freely available code from the Internet. Although this is obviously convenient, it is not risk-free. There are many examples of malicious code being distributed this way. In general, no third-party scripts should be installed on a Web server unless they are first subjected to a thorough code review by a trusted expert. Security code reviews should also be considered for content on Web servers that are critical to the organization or are highly threatened.

---

[42] For more extensive guidelines on active content, please see NIST SP 800-28 Version 2, *Guidelines on Active Content and Mobile Code* (http://csrc.nist.gov/publications/nistpubs/).

6.4.1 Vulnerabilities with Client-Side Active Content Technologies

Each active content technology has its own strengths and weaknesses; none is perfectly secure. Some of the more popular active content technologies and their associated risks are discussed below. New technologies are emerging all the time and older technologies are continually enhanced. Any Web administrator or Webmaster who is considering deploying a Web site with features that require active content technology on the client side should carefully weigh the risks and benefits of the technology before implementation. The relative risk of active content technologies changes over time, complicating this task. Nevertheless, common risks to the Web server prevail with all active content technologies. Because these technologies involve placing application code on the client, an attacker may attempt to reverse engineer the code to gain an understanding of how it functions with an organization's Web site and exploit that relationship. For example, relying only on input validation checks performed at the client by the active content and not validating the input again at the Web server would allow an attacker to use an HTTP proxy tool or editor to modify the active content elements and bypass any or all checks performed.

Java is a full-featured, object-oriented programming language compiled into platform-independent byte code executed by an interpreter called the Java Virtual Machine (JVM). The resulting byte code can be executed where compiled or transferred to another Java-enabled platform (e.g., conveyed via an HTML Web page as an applet). Java is useful for adding functionality to Web sites. Many services offered by various popular Web sites require the user to have a Java-enabled browser. When the Web browser sees references to Java code, the browser loads the code and processes it using the built-in JVM or a user-installed one.

The Java programming language and runtime environment enforce security primarily through strong type safety, by which a program can perform certain operations only on certain kinds of objects. Java follows a so-called sandbox security model, used to isolate memory and method access and to maintain mutually exclusive execution domains. Java code, such as a Web applet, is confined to a "sandbox," which is designed to prevent it from performing unauthorized operations, such as inspecting or changing files on a client file system and using network connections to circumvent file protections or users' expectations of privacy. Java byte code downloaded to the client can be decompiled into a more readable form by the user, making it susceptible to reverse engineering and possible modification, which poses a threat to the Web server.

Hostile applets can also pose security threats to the client, even while executing within the sandbox. A hostile applet can consume or exploit system resources inappropriately, or can cause a user to perform an undesired or unwanted action. Examples of hostile applet exploits include DoS, mail forging, invasion of privacy (e.g., exporting of identity, e-mail address, and platform information), and installing backdoors to the system. Because the Java security model is rather complex, it can be difficult for a user to understand and manage. This situation can increase risk. Moreover, many implementation bugs have also been found, enabling security mechanisms to be bypassed [NIST01].

JavaScript is a general purpose, cross-platform scripting language, whose code can be embedded within standard Web pages to create interactive documents. The name JavaScript is a misnomer because the language has little relationship to Java technology and was developed independently from it. Within the context of the Web browser, JavaScript is extremely powerful, allowing prepared scripts to perform essentially the same actions as those a user could take. Within that context, JavaScript lacks methods for directly accessing a client file system or for directly opening connections to computers other than the host that provided the content source. The browser also normally confines a script's execution to the page from which it was downloaded [NIST01].

In theory, confining a scripting language to the boundaries of a Web browser should provide a relatively secure environment. In practice, this has not been the case. Many attacks against browsers stem from the use of a scripting language in combination with exploitation of a security vulnerability. The sources of most problems have been twofold: the prevalence of implementation flaws in the execution environment and the close binding of the browser to other functionality, such as an e-mail client. Past exploits include sending a user's URL history list to a remote site and using the mail address of the user to forge e-mails [NIST01]. Client-side JavaScript can also be read and analyzed by an attacker to identify possible vulnerabilities in the Web server.

Adobe Flash is a browser plug-in for major Web browsers that provides support for improved animation and interactivity. Although plug-ins such as Flash allow browsers to support new types of content, they are not active content in and of themselves, but simply an active-content-enabling technology. The Flash plug-in allows browsers to support vector and raster graphics, streaming audio and video, and ActionScript, a programming language similar to JavaScript used to control Flash animations. Several versions of Flash contain security flaws that allow remote code execution, requiring users to apply patches to the plug-in.

Adobe Shockwave is a browser plug-in similar to Adobe Flash but more robust. Shockwave provides a faster rendering engine and supports hardware-accelerated three-dimensional graphics, layered graphics, and network protocols. While Flash is widely used for Web animations and movies, Shockwave is commonly used for games. As with Flash, several versions of Shockwave contain security flaws that allow remote code execution, requiring users to apply patches to the plug-in.

AJAX is a collection of technologies that allows Web developers to improve the response times between Web pages. JavaScript code communicates with the Web server and dynamically modifies the contents of the Web browser's page without relying on the Web server to send a response with the XML markup for the entire page. Instead, only the required portion of the affected XML data is transmitted. AJAX allows Web content to behave more like traditional applications, while potentially reducing the load on the Web server. However, a number of security concerns exist with AJAX:

■ AJAX creates a larger attack surface than traditional Web applications by increasing the number of points where a client interacts with the application.

■ AJAX may reveal details of internal functions within the Web application.

■ Some AJAX endpoints may not require authentication and instead rely on the current state of the application [SPID06].

Visual Basic Script (VBScript) is a programming language developed by Microsoft for creating scripts that can be embedded in Web pages for viewing with the Internet Explorer browser. However, other browsers do not necessarily support VBScript. Like JavaScript, VBScript is an interpreted language that can process client-side scripts. VBScript, which is a subset of the Microsoft Visual Basic programming language, works with Microsoft ActiveX controls. The language is similar to JavaScript and poses similar risks.

ActiveX is a set of technologies from Microsoft that provide tools for linking desktop applications to the Web. ActiveX controls are reusable component program objects that can be attached to e-mail or downloaded from a Web site. ActiveX controls also come preinstalled on Windows platforms. Web pages invoke ActiveX controls using a scripting language or with an HTML OBJECT tag. ActiveX controls are compiled program objects, making them difficult to read and reverse engineer.

Unlike the Java sandbox model, which restricts the permissions of applets to a set of safe actions, ActiveX places no restrictions on what a control can do. Instead, ActiveX controls are digitally signed by their authors under a technology scheme called Authenticode. The digital signatures are verified using identity certificates issued by a trusted certificate authority to an ActiveX software publisher, who must pledge that no harmful code will be knowingly distributed under this scheme. The Authenticode process ensures that ActiveX controls cannot be distributed anonymously and that tampering with the controls can be detected. This certification process, however, does not ensure that a control will be well behaved [NIST01]. Vulnerabilities in key ActiveX controls have been reported, including components installed by popular applications such as Microsoft Office.

6.4.2 Vulnerabilities with Server-Side Content Generation Technologies

Unlike the above technologies, CGI, ASP .NET, Java EE, and other similar server interfaces fall on the server side (Web) of the client-server model. Common uses of server-side execution include [Ziri02]—

■ Database access

■ E-commerce/e-government applications

■ Chat rooms

■ Threaded discussion groups.

The server-side applications can be written in many programming languages to run on a Web server. If scripts and components are not prepared carefully, however, attackers can find and exercise flaws in the code to penetrate the Web server or backend components such as a database server. Therefore, scripts must be written with security in mind; for example, they should not run arbitrary commands on a system or launch insecure programs. An attacker can find flaws through trial and error and does not necessarily need the source code for the script to uncover vulnerabilities [NIST01].

Server-side content generators can create the following security vulnerabilities at the server:

■ They may intentionally or unintentionally leak information about the Web server application and host OS that can aid an attacker, for example, by allowing access to information outside the areas designated for Web use.

■ When processing user-provided input, such as the contents of a form, URL parameters, or a search query, they may be vulnerable to attacks whereby the user tricks the application into executing arbitrary commands supplied in the input stream (e.g., cross-site scripting or SQL injection).

■ They may allow attackers to deface or modify site content.

Ideally, server-side applications should constrain users to a small set of well-defined functionality and validate the size and values of input parameters so that an attacker cannot overrun memory boundaries or piggyback arbitrary commands for execution. Applications should be run only with minimal privileges (i.e., non-administrator) to avoid compromising the entire Web site. However, potential security holes can be exploited, even when applications run with low privilege settings, so this option should only be used as a last resort. For example, a subverted script could have enough privileges to mail out the system password file, examine the network information maps, or launch a login to a high numbered port.

The areas of vulnerability mentioned potentially affect all Web servers. Although these vulnerabilities have frequently occurred with CGI applications, other related interfaces and techniques for developing server applications have not been immune. CGI, being an early and well-supported standard, has simply gained more attention over the years, and the same areas of vulnerability exist when applying similar Web development technologies.

CGI scripts were the initial mechanism used to make Web sites interact with databases and other applications. However, as the Web evolved, server-side processing methods have been developed that are more efficient and easier to program; for example, Microsoft provides ASP.NET for its IIS servers, Sun/Netscape supports Java servlets, and the freeware PHP is supported by most major Web platforms, including Apache and IIS [NIST01]. Some important points to consider when contemplating the deployment of CGI [Ziri02]:

■ The host file system (see Section 4.1) provides security for CGI.

■ Most servers allow per-directory CGI restrictions.

■ CGI itself provides little security enforcement.

■ Perl facilitates secure programming that most other languages (e.g., C, C++, sh) do not.

■ CGI wrappers available from third parties offer additional protection for CGI.

Server Side Includes (SSI) is a limited server-side scripting language supported by most Web servers. SSI provides a set of dynamic features, including the current time or the last modification date of the HTML file, as an alternative to using a CGI program to perform the function. When the browser requests a document with a special file type, such as ".shtml", it triggers the server to treat the document as a template, reading and parsing the entire document before sending the results back to the client (Web browser). SSI commands are embedded within HTML comments (e.g., <!--#include file="standard.html" -->). As the server reads the template file, it searches for HTML comments containing embedded SSI commands. When it finds one, the server replaces that part of the original HTML text with the output of the command. For example, the SSI command given above (i.e., #include file) replaces the entire SSI comment with the contents of another HTML file. This allows the display of a corporate logo or other static information prepared in another file to occur in a uniform way across all corporate Web pages. A subset of the directives available allows the server to execute arbitrary system commands and CGI scripts, which may produce unwanted side effects [NIST01]. Some important points to consider when contemplating the deployment of SSIs:

■ The security of SSIs is extremely weak if the exec command is enabled on the Web server.

■ The impact of SSIs can hurt the performance of heavily loaded Web servers.

■ The security of SSIs relies heavily on the host OS and Web server application for security.

Microsoft ASP.NET is a server-side scripting technology from Microsoft that can be used to create dynamic and interactive Web applications. An ASP page contains server-side scripts that run when a browser requests an ".asp" resource from the Web server. The Web server processes the requested page and executes any script commands encountered before sending a generated HTML page to the user's browser. Both C# and VBScript are natively supported as ASP.NET scripting languages, but other languages can be accommodated, if an ASP.NET-compliant interpreter for the language is installed. For example, ASP.NET engines are available for the Perl, REXX, and Python languages from various sources. The following are some important points to consider when contemplating the deployment of ASP.NET [Ziri02]:

■ ASP.NET relies heavily on the host OS and Web server application for security.

■ Client security is well integrated with Web server and host OS authentication services.

■ ASP.NET supports Microsoft Code Access Security, which provides methods for the content developer or administrator to constrain privileges.

■ ASP.NET is relatively immune to buffer overflows.

■ ASP.NET is a well-documented and mature technology.

Java EE is based on Java technology (see Section 6.4.1) and provides a type of server-side applet called a servlet. The Web server first determines whether the browser's request requires dynamically generated information from a servlet, which processes the request and generates an HTTP response, a Java Server Page (JSP), or a static HTML page. If a servlet is required, the Web server can then locate or instantiate a servlet object corresponding to the request and invoke it to obtain the needed results. If a JSP is requested, Java EE compiles the JSP into a servlet, then instantiates and invokes it to obtain a response. If a static HTML page is requested, Java EE simply returns the HTML content like a traditional Web server.

The Java EE server typically populates itself with the servlet objects, which remain inactive until invoked. Thus, little or no startup overhead is associated with execution of the servlet objects. A Web server may also offload the handling of servlets to another server. By relying on Java portability and observing a common API, servlet objects can run in nearly any server environment. Servlets allow developers to take advantage of an object-oriented environment on the Web server, which is flexible and extendible. Moreover, untrusted servlet objects can be executed in a secure area, with the dynamically generated information being passed from the secure area into the remaining server environment [NIST01].

Some important points to consider when contemplating the deployment of Java servlets [Ziri02]:

■ Java EE is tightly integrated with host OS security and Web server authentication for strong security.

■ Java EE facilitates secure programming by—

   ■ Leveraging security of Java language

   ■ Using a strong security model supporting constraints by developers and server administrators

   ■ Employing secure error handling.

■ Java EE is a well-documented and mature technology.

■ A large amount of robust third-party code from IBM, Sun, Apache Foundation, and other developers is available for use with Java EE.

PHP is a scripting language used to create dynamic Web pages. With syntax from C, Java, and Perl, PHP code is embedded within HTML pages for server-side execution. PHP is commonly used to extract data from a database and present it on a Web page. Most major Windows and Unix Web servers support the language, and it is widely used with the mySQL database [NIST01]. The following are some important points to consider when contemplating the deployment of PHP:

■ The latest version of PHP available should be used because older versions have numerous security vulnerabilities.

■ PHP provides a number of options that simplify development; some of these options (e.g., the *register_globals* option, which converts all input parameters into PHP variables and may override values in the PHP script) can make it more difficult for novices to develop secure programs.

■ Much of the freely available third-party code for PHP is poorly written from a security perspective.[43]

6.4.3 Server-Side Content Generator Security Considerations

When examining or writing an active content executable or script, consider the following:

■ The executable code should be as simple as possible. The longer or more complex it is, the more likely it will have problems.

■ The executable code's ability to read and write programs should be limited. Code that reads files may inadvertently violate access restrictions or pass sensitive system information. Code that writes files may modify or damage documents or introduce Trojan horses.

■ The code's interaction with other programs or applications should be analyzed to identify security vulnerabilities. For example, many CGI scripts send e-mails in response to form input by opening up a connection with the sendmail program. Ensure this interaction is performed in a secure manner.

■ On Linux/Unix hosts, the code should not run with suid (set-user-id).

■ The code should use explicit path names when invoking external programs. Relying on the PATH environment variable to resolve partial path names is not recommended.

■ Web servers should be scanned periodically for vulnerabilities, even if they do not employ active content (see Section 9.4.1). Network security scanners may detect vulnerabilities in the Web server, OS, or other services running on the Web server. Web application vulnerability scanners specifically scan for content generator vulnerabilities (see Appendix C for more information).

■ Web content generation code should be scanned and/or audited (depending on the sensitivity of the Web server and its content). Commercially available tools can scan .NET or Java code. A number of commercial entities offer code review services.

■ Web content generation code should be developed following current recommended practices.[44]

■ For data entry forms, determine a list of expected characters and filter out unexpected characters from input data entered by a user before processing a form. For example, on most forms, expected data

---

[43] There are a number of reasons for the poor security of many PHP scripts. The most obvious is that many scripts are written without concern for security. In addition, because of the relative ease of coding PHP scripts, many novices who have little knowledge of secure programming create and often freely distribute poorly written scripts.

[44] OWASP is compiling a guide containing Web application development best practices on their site at http://www.owasp.org/index.php/OWASP_Guide_Project.

falls in these categories: letters a-z, A-Z, and 0-9. Care should be taken when accepting special characters such as &, ', ", @, and !. These symbols may have special meanings within the content generation language or other components of the Web application.

■ Ensure that the dynamically generated pages do not contain dangerous metacharacters. It is possible for a malicious user to place these tags in a database or a file. When a dynamic page is generated using the altered data, the malicious code embedded in the tags may be passed to the client browser. Then the user's browser can be tricked into running a program of the attacker's choice. This program will execute in the browser's security context for communicating with the legitimate Web server, not the browser's security context for communicating with the attacker. Thus, the program will execute in an inappropriate security context with inappropriate privileges.

■ Character set encoding should be explicitly set in each page. Then the user data should be scanned for byte sequences that represent special characters for the given encoding scheme.

■ Each character in a specified character set can be encoded using its numeric value. Encoding the output can be used as an alternate for filtering the data. Encoding becomes especially important when special characters, such as copyright symbols, can be part of the dynamic data. However, encoding data can be resource intensive, and a balance must be struck between encoding and other methods for filtering the data.

■ Cookies should be examined for any special characters. Any special characters should be filtered out.

■ An encryption mechanism should be used to encrypt passwords entered through script forms (see Section 7.5).

■ For Web applications that are restricted by username and password, none of the Web pages in the application should be accessible without executing the appropriate login process.

■ Many Web servers and some other Web server software install sample scripts or executables during the installation process. Many of these have known vulnerabilities and should be removed immediately. See appropriate manufacturer's documentation or Web sites for more information.

When considering a server-side content generator, it is important to review public vulnerability and security databases (such as NVD, http://nvd.nist.gov/) to determine the relative risk of the various technologies under consideration. Although the historical record will not be a perfect indicator of future risk, it does indicate which technologies appear to be more vulnerable.

Various organizations research network and system security topics and periodically publish information concerning recently discovered vulnerabilities in software. This includes Web server software and supporting technologies, such as scripting languages and external programs. External programs that are in wide use are regularly analyzed by researchers, users, and security incident response teams and by attackers. Attackers will often publish exploit scripts that take advantage of known vulnerabilities in Web service software and external programs commonly used by public Web servers. Web administrators should review public information sources frequently and be aware of all security-relevant information about any external programs that they are considering.

6.4.4 Location of Server-Side Content Generators

The location of active content on the Web server is critical. If located in an incorrect directory or in a directory with the wrong permissions, it can quickly lead to the compromise of the Web server. To avoid this problem—

■ Writable files should be identified and placed in separate folders. No script files should exist in writable folders. As an example, guest book data is usually saved in simple text files. These files need write permissions for guests to be able to submit their comments.

■ Executable files (e.g., CGI, .EXE, .CMD, and PL) should be placed in separate folders. No other readable or writable documents should be placed in these folders.

■ Script files (e.g., ASP, PHP, and PL) should have separate folders. It may also be beneficial to store the scripts in a folder with a non-obvious name (e.g., not "Scripts") to make it more difficult for an attacker to find the scripts through direct browsing.

■ Include files (e.g., INC, SHTML, SHTM, and ASP) created for code reusability should be placed in separate directories. SSI should not generally be used on public Web servers. ASP include files should have an .asp extension instead of .inc. Note that much of the risk with include files is in their execute capability. If the execute capability is disabled, this risk is drastically reduced.

6.4.5 Cross-Site Scripting Vulnerabilities

Cross-site scripting (XSS) is a vulnerability typically found in interactive Web applications that allows code injection by malicious Web users into the Web pages viewed by other users. It generally occurs in Web pages that do not do the appropriate bounds checking on data input by users. An exploited cross-site scripting vulnerability can be used by attackers to compromise other users' computers or to receive data from another user's Web session (e.g., user ID and password or session cookie). Thus, although this is a client side exploit, it also impacts the server indirectly since a compromised user, particularly one with elevated privileges, represents a threat to the server. XSS vulnerabilities are used frequently to conduct phishing attacks or exploit Web browser vulnerabilities to gain control of end user PCs.

XSS vulnerabilities are highly varied and frequently unique to a particular Web application. They encompass two general categories:

■ **Persistent** XSS vulnerabilities allow for the more powerful attacks. This vulnerability occurs when data provided to a Web application by an untrusted user is stored persistently on the server and displayed to other users as Web content but is not validated or encoded using HTML. A common example of this is online message boards, wikis, and blogs where users are allowed to post HTML-formatted messages for other users to view. In this example, after a malicious user posts a malicious message or reply, any other user who accesses a page displaying that data and whose browser is vulnerable to the exploit can be compromised.

■ **Non-persistent** XSS vulnerabilities, sometimes called reflected, are more common and somewhat less dangerous than persistent vulnerabilities. Non-persistent vulnerabilities occur when data provided by a Web client is used immediately by server-side scripts to generate a results page for that user (e.g., login screen, search results page). If the unvalidated client-supplied data is included in the returned page without any HTML encoding, this will allow client-side code to be injected into the dynamic page. This might not appear to be a problem on the surface, since an attacker can only exploit himself or herself. However, an attacker could send a specially crafted URL to a user and trick the user through social engineering into clicking on the maliciously crafted URL. If the user's Web browser was vulnerable to the exploit, the user's machine could be compromised. Since this attack does require some level social engineering, it is considered somewhat less dangerous than attacks on persistent vulnerabilities.

The solution to XSS attacks is to validate all user input and remove any unexpected or potentially risky data. Another solution is to use an HTML-quoted version[45] of any user input that is presented back to other users. This will prevent the Web browsers of other users from interpreting that input and acting on any embedded commands present.

6.5 Checklist for Securing Web Content

Completed	Action
	Ensure that none of the following types of information are available on or through a public Web server
☐	Classified records
☐	Internal personnel rules and procedures
☐	Sensitive or proprietary information
☐	Personal information about an organization's personnel
☐	Telephone numbers, e-mail addresses, or general listings of staff unless necessary to fulfill organizational requirements
☐	Schedules of organizational principals or their exact location (whether on or off the premises)
☐	Information on the composition, preparation, or optimal use of hazardous materials or toxins
☐	Sensitive information relating to homeland security
☐	Investigative records
☐	Financial records (beyond those already publicly available)
☐	Medical records
☐	Organization's physical and information security procedures
☐	Information about organization's network and information system infrastructure
☐	Information that specifies or implies physical security vulnerabilities
☐	Plans, maps, diagrams, aerial photographs, and architectural plans of organizational building, properties, or installations
☐	Copyrighted material without the written permission of the owner
☐	Privacy or security policies that indicate the types of security measures in place to the degree that they may be useful to an attacker
	Establish an organizational-wide documented formal policy and process for approving public Web content that—
☐	Identifies information that should be published on the Web
☐	Identifies target audience
☐	Identifies possible negative ramifications of publishing the information
☐	Identifies who should be responsible for creating, publishing, and maintaining this particular information

---

[45] More information on HTML quoting is available at http://www.w3.org/TR/html4/charset.html#entities and http://www.w3.org/TR/html4/sgml/entities.html.

Completed	Action
☐	Provides guidelines on styles and formats appropriate for Web publishing
☐	Provides for appropriate review of the information for sensitivity and distribution/release controls (including the sensitivity of the information in aggregate)
☐	Determines the appropriate access and security controls
☐	Provides guidance on the information contained within the source code of the Web content
	Maintain Web user privacy
☐	Maintain a published privacy policy
☐	Prohibit the collection of personally identifying data without the explicit permission of the user and collect only the data that is absolutely needed
☐	Prohibit the use of "persistent" cookies
☐	Use the session cookie only if it is clearly identified in published privacy policy
	Mitigate indirect attacks on content
☐	Ensure users of the site are aware of the dangers of phishing and pharming attacks and how to avoid them
☐	Validate official communication by personalizing emails and providing unique identifying (but not confidential) information only the organization and user should know
☐	Use digital signatures on e-mail if appropriate
☐	Perform content validation within the Web application to prevent more sophisticated phishing attacks (e.g., cross-site scripting based attacks)
☐	Personalize Web content to aid in users' identifying fraudulent Web sites
☐	Use token-based or mutual authentication if applicable
☐	Suggest the use of Web browsers or browser toolbars with phishing/pharming protection
☐	Use current versions of DNS software with the latest security patches
☐	Install server-side DNS protection mechanisms
☐	Monitor organizational domains and similar domains
☐	Simplify the structure of organization domain names
☐	Use secure connections for logins
☐	If necessary, engage a vendor to provide stronger anti-phishing/anti-pharming measures
	Client-side active content security considerations
☐	Weigh the risks and benefits of client-side active content
☐	Take no actions without the express permission of user
☐	When possible, only use widely-adopted active content such as JavaScript, PDF, and Flash
☐	When possible, provide alternatives (e.g., HTML provided along with PDF)
	Maintain server-side active content security
☐	Only simple, easy-to-understand code should be used
☐	Limited or no reading or writing to the file system should be permitted
☐	Limited or no interaction with other programs (e.g., sendmail) should be permitted
☐	There should be no requirement to run with suid privileges on Unix or Linux
☐	Explicit path names should be used (i.e., does not rely on path variable)

Completed	Action
☐	No directories have both write and execute permissions
☐	All executable files are placed in a dedicated folders
☐	SSIs are disabled or the execute function is disabled
☐	All user input is validated
☐	Web content generation code should be scanned or audited
☐	Dynamically created pages do not create dangerous metacharacters
☐	Character set encoding should be explicitly set in each page
☐	User data should be scanned to ensure it contains only expected input, (e.g., a-z, A-Z, 0-9); care should be taken with special characters or HTML tags
☐	Cookies should be examined for any special characters
☐	Encryption mechanism is used to encrypt passwords entered through scripts forms
☐	For Web applications that are restricted by username and password, none of the Web pages in the application should be accessible without executing the appropriate login process
☐	All sample scripts are removed
☐	No third-party scripts or executable code are used without verifying the source code

7. Using Authentication and Encryption Technologies

Public Web servers often support a range of technologies for identifying and authenticating users with differing privileges for accessing information. Some of these technologies are based on cryptographic functions that can provide an encrypted channel between a Web browser client and a Web server that supports encryption.

Without user authentication, organizations will not be able to restrict access to specific information to authorized users. All information that resides on a public Web server will then be accessible by anyone with access to the server. In addition, without some process to authenticate the server, users will not be able to determine if the server is the "authentic" Web server or a counterfeit version operated by a malicious entity.

Encryption can be used to protect information traversing the connection between a Web browser client and a public Web server. Without encryption, anyone with access to the network traffic can determine, and possibly alter, the content of sensitive information, even if the user accessing the information has been authenticated carefully. This may violate the confidentiality and integrity of critical information.

7.1 Determining Authentication and Encryption Requirements

Organizations should periodically examine all information accessible on the public Web server and determine the necessary security requirements. While doing so, the organization should identify information that shares the same security and protection requirements. For sensitive information, the organization should determine the users or user groups that should have access to each set of resources.

For information that requires some level of user authentication, the organization should determine which of the following technologies or methods would provide the appropriate level of authentication and encryption. Each has its own unique benefits and costs that should be weighed carefully with client and organizational requirements and policies. It may be desirable to use some authentication methods in combination.

This guide discusses the authentication mechanisms most commonly associated with public Web servers and Web applications. More advanced authentication mechanisms can be supported by these servers and applications and are discussed in NIST SP 800-63.[46]

7.2 Address-Based Authentication

The simplest authentication mechanism that is supported by most Web servers is address-based authentication. Access control is based on the IP address and/or hostname of the host requesting information. Although it is easy to implement for small groups of users, address authentication can be unwieldy for Web sites that have a large potential user population (i.e., most public Web servers). It is susceptible to several types of attacks, including IP spoofing and DNS poisoning. This type of authentication should be used only where minimal security is required, unless it is used in conjunction with stronger authentication methods.

---

[46] NIST SP 800-63, *Electronic Authentication Guideline*, is available at http://csrc.nist.gov/publications/nistpubs/.

7.3 Basic Authentication

The basic authentication technology uses the Web server content's directory structure. Typically, all files in the same directory are configured with the same access privileges. A requesting user provides a recognized user identification and password for access to files in a given directory. More restrictive access control can be enforced at the level of a single file within a directory if the Web server software provides this capability. Each vendor's Web server software has its own method and syntax for defining and using this basic authentication mechanism.

From a security perspective, the main drawback of this technology is that all password information is transferred in an encoded, rather than an encrypted, form. Anyone who knows the standardized encoding scheme can decode the password after capturing it with a network sniffer. Furthermore, any Web content is transmitted as unencrypted plaintext, so this content also can be captured, violating confidentiality. These limitations can be overcome using basic authentication in conjunction with SSL/TLS (see Section 7.5). Basic authentication is supported by standard-compliant Web browsers [Koss00]. Basic authentication is useful for protecting information from malicious bots (see Section 5.2.4) because the bots should not have the necessary credentials to access the protected directories. However, this mechanism should not be considered secure against more determined and sophisticated attackers.

7.4 Digest Authentication

Because of the drawbacks with basic authentication, an improved technique known as digest authentication was introduced in version 1.1 of the HTTP protocol.[47] Digest authentication uses a challenge-response mechanism for user authentication. Under this approach, a nonce or arbitrary value is sent to the user, who is prompted for an ID and password, as with basic authentication. However, in this case, the information entered by the user is concatenated and a cryptographic hash of the result is formed. This hash is concatenated with the nonce and a hash of the requested method and URL, and the result is then rehashed as a response value that is sent to the server.

Because the user's password is not sent in the clear, it cannot be directly sniffed from the network. The user's password is not needed by the server to authenticate the user—only the hashed value of the user ID and password. Because the nonce can serve as an indicator of timeliness (e.g., it can be composed of date and time information), replay attacks are also thwarted. Unfortunately, all other information is sent in the clear and is vulnerable to interception and alteration. Digest authentication is also susceptible to offline dictionary attacks (see Section 7.6) where the attacker tries various passwords in an attempt to recreate the captured digest value. These limitations can be overcome using digest authentication in conjunction with SSL/TLS (see Section 7.5).[48] Like basic authentication, digest authentication is useful for protecting information from malicious bots (see Section 5.2.4).

---

[47] More information on basic and digest authentication is available from IETF RFC 2617, *HTTP Authentication: Basic and Digest Access Authentication* (http://www.ietf.org/rfc/rfc2617.txt).

[48] For example, offline dictionary attacks can be performed against intercepted digest authentication passwords to identify the cleartext passwords. Intercepted digest authentication passwords that are sent over SSL-protected connections are not susceptible to offline dictionary attacks.

7.5 SSL/TLS

The SSL and TLS protocols provide server and client authentication and encryption of communications.[49] SSL was first introduced by Netscape Communications in 1994 and was revised twice (SSL version 3 is the current version).[50] In 1996, the Internet Engineering Task Force (IETF) established the TLS working group to formalize and advance the SSL protocol to the level of Internet standard. The TLS protocol version 1.0 is formally specified in IETF Request for Comments (RFC) 2246,[51] which was published in 1999 and is based in large part on SSL version 3. SSL version 3 and TLS version 1 are essentially identical and are discussed together in this document. Most major Internet components, such as Web browsers, support the use of both SSL 3 and TLS 1.0. TLS 1.1, specified in RFC 4436, was released in April 2006, and future versions of Web browsers will likely support it.

TCP/IP governs the transport and routing of data over the Internet. Other protocols, such as HTTP, LDAP, and Internet Message Access Protocol (IMAP), run "on top of" TCP/IP in that they all use TCP/IP to support typical application tasks, such as displaying Web pages or delivering e-mail messages. Thus, SSL/TLS can support more than just secure Web communications. Figure 7-1 shows how SSL/TLS fits between the application and network/transport layers of the Internet protocol suite.

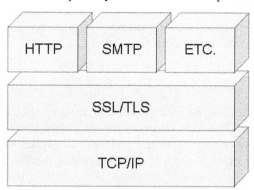

Figure 7-1. SSL/TLS Location within the Internet Protocol Stack

7.5.1 SSL/TLS Capabilities

SSL/TLS provides the following capabilities to HTTP and other application layer protocols [SSL98]:

■ **Server Authentication**—SSL/TLS allows a Web client (user) to confirm a Web server's identity. SSL/TLS-enabled Web clients (browsers) can employ standard techniques of public key cryptography to check that a server's name and public key are contained in a valid certificate issued by a CA listed in the client's list of trusted CAs. This confirmation might be important if the user, for example, is sending a credit card number over the network and wants to confirm the receiving server's identity.

■ **Client Authentication**—SSL/TLS allows a Web server to confirm a user's identity using the same techniques as those used for server authentication by reversing the roles. SSL/TLS-enabled Web

---

[49] Proper understanding of SSL and the information presented in this section requires at least a basic understanding of cryptographic algorithms, message digest functions, digital signatures, symmetric encryption algorithms, and asymmetric encryption algorithms. For an introduction to cryptography, see NIST SP 800-32, *Introduction to Public Key Technology and the Federal PKI Infrastructure*. For more information on transport layer security, see NIST SP 800-52, *Guidelines for the Selection and Use of Transport Layer Security (TLS) Implementations*. Both of these documents can be found at http://csrc.nist.gov/publications/nistpubs/.

[50] SSL versions before 3.0 are insecure and should not be used.

[51] http://www.ietf.org/rfc/rfc2246.txt

server software can confirm that a client's certificate is valid and was issued by a CA listed in the server's list of trusted CAs.[52] This confirmation might be important if the server, for example, is a bank that is sending confidential financial information to a customer and wants to confirm the recipient's identity.[53] If client authentication is to be performed, server authentication must also be performed.

■ **Communication Encryption**—SSL/TLS can encrypt most of the information being transmitted between a Web browser (client) and a Web server or even between two Web servers. With an appropriate encryption algorithm, SSL/TLS provides a high degree of confidentiality. In addition, all data sent over an encrypted SSL/TLS connection is protected with a mechanism for detecting tampering; that is, for automatically determining if the data has been altered in transit.

7.5.2 Weaknesses of SSL/TLS

Several limitations are inherent with SSL/TLS. Packets are encrypted at the TCP layer, so IP layer information is not encrypted. Although this protects the Web data being transmitted, a person monitoring an SSL/TLS session can determine both the sender and receiver via the unencrypted IP address information. In addition, SSL/TLS only protects data while it is being transmitted, not when it is stored at either endpoint. Thus, the data is still vulnerable while in storage (e.g., a credit card database) unless additional safeguards are taken at the endpoints.

If SSL/TLS is implemented or used incorrectly, the communications intended to be protected may be vulnerable to a "man in the middle" attack. This occurs when a malicious entity intercepts all communication between the Web client and the Web server with which the client is attempting to establish an SSL/TLS connection. The attacker intercepts the legitimate keys that are passed back and forth during the SSL/TLS handshake (see Section 7.5.3) and substitutes the attacker's keys, making it appear to the Web client that the attacker is the Web server and to the Web server that the attacker is the Web client [SSL98]. If SSL/TLS is implemented and used properly, it is not susceptible to man-in-the-middle attacks.

The encrypted information exchanged at the beginning of the SSL/TLS handshake is actually encrypted with the malicious entity's public key or private key, rather than the Web client's or Web server's real keys. The attacker program ends up establishing one set of session keys for use with the real Web server, and a different set of session keys for use with the Web client. This allows the attacker program not only to read all the data that flows between the Web client and the real Web server but also to change the data without being detected. This threat can be mitigated if clients rely upon server certificates issued by trusted CAs or on self-signed certificates obtained by secure mechanisms. Presentation of a self-signed certificate may be an indication that a man-in-the-middle attack is underway. Browsers may perform some checks automatically, but they cannot be relied upon in all instances.

Even without performing a man-in-the-middle attack, attackers may attempt to trick users into accessing an invalid Web site. There are several possible methods for attack, including—

■ Presenting a self-signed certificate unknown to the user and getting the user to accept it as legitimate. Although the Web browser can be configured to display a warning when a self-signed certificate is

[52] Servers and clients use different types of certificates for authentication; specifically, clients have to be authenticated using a signature certificate. See Section 7.5.3 for additional information.
[53] Client authentication performed by SSL/TLS is rarely used for public Web servers because of the logistics involved in providing client certificates to users and having them installed correctly for use by Web browsers.

presented, organizations that rely on self-signed certificates might instruct users to ignore such warnings.

■ Exploiting vulnerabilities in a Web browser so that the Web site appears to be valid to an untrained user

■ Taking advantage of a cross-site scripting vulnerability on a legitimate Web site. The Web browser will be accessing two different sites, but it will appear to the user that only the legitimate site is being accessed.

■ Taking advantage of the certificate approval process to receive a valid certificate and apply it to the attacker's own site. By using a valid certificate on what appears to be a valid site, the certificate will validate, and the user would have to somehow realize that the site being accessed is malicious.

SSL spoofing attacks can occur without requiring any user intervention. As a proof of concept in 2005, the Shmoo Group registered an internationalized domain name that looked similar to a valid site when displayed in a browser. The SSL certificate matched the internationalized domain name of the Web site, so no user warning occurred. In the address bar, the URL appeared almost identical to that of the original spoofed Web site [NVD06].

Users can prevent less sophisticated attacks by confirming the validity of a certificate[54] before relying on the security of an SSL/TLS session and rejecting certificates for which the browser presents warnings.[55] Browsers perform some checks automatically, but they cannot be relied upon in all instances.

7.5.3   Example SSL/TLS Session

The SSL/TLS protocols use a combination of public key and symmetric key encryption. Symmetric key encryption is much faster than public key encryption, whereas public key encryption is better suited to provide authentication and establish symmetric keys. An SSL/TLS session always begins with an exchange of messages called the SSL/TLS handshake. The handshake allows the server to authenticate itself to the client using public key techniques; this allows the client and the server to cooperate in the creation of symmetric keys used for rapid encryption, decryption, and tamper detection during the session that follows. The handshake also allows the client to authenticate itself to the server.

The exact programmatic details of the messages exchanged during the SSL/TLS handshake are beyond the scope of this document. However, the basic steps involved can be summarized as follows [SSL98]:

1.   "The client sends the server the client's SSL/TLS version number, cipher settings, randomly generated data, and other information the server needs to communicate with the client using SSL/TLS."

2.   "The server sends the client the server's SSL/TLS version number, cipher settings, randomly generated data, and other information the client needs to communicate with the server over SSL/TLS. The server also sends its own certificate and, if the client is requesting a server resource that requires client authentication, requests the client's certificate."

---

[54]   Checking a certificate using most Web browsers involves clicking on a padlock icon in the lower right-hand corner of the browser (this icon will only appear when accessing an SSL/TLS-protected resource).

[55]   When organizations use self-signed certificates and instruct users to accept them, it may encourage users to do so with potentially malicious certificates.

3. "The client uses some of the information sent by the server to authenticate the server. If the server cannot be authenticated, the user is warned of the problem and informed that an encrypted and authenticated connection cannot be established. If the server can be successfully authenticated, the client goes on to Step 4."

4. "Using all data generated in the handshake to this point, the client (with the cooperation of the server, depending on the cipher being used) creates the premaster secret for the session, encrypts it with the server's public key (obtained from the server's certificate, sent in Step 2), and sends the encrypted premaster secret to the server."

5. "If the server has requested client authentication (an optional step in the handshake), the client also signs another piece of data that is unique to this handshake and known by both the client and server. In this case, the client sends both the signed data and the client's own certificate to the server, along with the encrypted premaster secret."

6. "If the server has requested client authentication, the server attempts to authenticate the client. If the client cannot be authenticated, the session is terminated. If the client can be successfully authenticated, the server uses its private key to decrypt the premaster secret, then performs a series of steps (which the client also performs, starting from the same premaster secret) to generate the master secret."

7. "Both the client and the server use the master secret to generate the session keys, which are symmetric keys used to encrypt and decrypt information exchanged during the SSL/TLS session and to verify its integrity—that is, to detect any changes in the data between the time it was sent and the time it is received over the SSL/TLS connection."

8. "The client sends a message to the server informing it that future messages from the client will be encrypted with the session key. It then sends a separate (encrypted) message indicating that the client portion of the handshake is finished."

9. "The server sends a message to the client informing it that future messages from the server will be encrypted with the session key. It then sends a separate (encrypted) message indicating that the server portion of the handshake is finished."

10. "The SSL/TLS handshake is now complete, and the SSL/TLS session has begun. The client and the server use the session keys to encrypt and decrypt the data they send to each other and to validate its integrity."

7.5.4 SSL/TLS Encryption Schemes

The SSL/TLS protocols support the use of a variety of different cryptographic algorithms for operations such as authenticating the Web server and Web client to each other, transmitting certificates, and establishing session keys. Web clients and Web servers may support different cipher suites, or sets of ciphers, depending on factors such as the versions of SSL/TLS they support; organizational policies regarding acceptable encryption strength; and government restrictions on export, import, and use of SSL/TLS-enabled software. Among other functions, the SSL/TLS handshake protocols determine how the Web server and Web client negotiate which cipher suites they will use to authenticate each other, transmit certificates, and establish session keys. Table 7-1 provides a list of Federal cipher suites, their recommended usage, and their relative strength [SSL98 and Chow02].

Table 7-1. SSL/TLS Cipher Suites

Recommended Use	Cipher Suites	Server Certificate
Highest Security	Encryption: Advanced Encryption Standard (AES) 128-bit or higher encryption[56], with fallback to Triple Data Encryption Standard (3DES) 168-bit encryption (using three keys)[57] HMAC: Secure Hash Algorithm 1 (SHA-1) or SHA-256 [58] Authentication: Digital Signature Standard (DSS) or RSA	DSS or RSA with a key size of 2048 bits or higher, and SHA-1 or SHA-256 hash function. Note that use of SHA-256 in certificates may cause incompatibilities with older clients.
Security and Performance	Encryption: AES 128-bit encryption HMAC: SHA-1 Authentication: DSS or RSA	DSS or RSA with a key size of 1024 bits or higher and SHA-1.
Security and Compatibility	Encryption: AES 128-bit encryption with fallback to Triple DES) 168-bit encryption (using three keys) HMAC: SHA-1 Authentication: DSS or RSA	DSS or RSA with a key size of 1024 bits or higher and SHA-1.
Authentication and Tamper Detection	HMAC: SHA-1 Authentication: DSS or RSA	DSS or RSA with a key size of 1024 bits or higher and SHA-1.

The server certificate used in the SSL/TSL handshake (described in more detail in Section 7.5.5) specifies the algorithm the certificate's public key supports, the public key, and the key size. The certificate may also describe its intended use (e.g., for generating digital signatures, encryption, or authentication). During the handshake phase, the client indicates the cipher suites and key lengths it supports. Ultimately, the choice of cipher suite and key length is dictated by the server.

Choosing an appropriate encryption algorithm depends on several factors that vary for each organization. Although at first glance it might appear that the strongest encryption available should always be used, that is not always true. The higher the level of the encryption, the greater impact it will have on the Web server's resources and communications speed.[59] Furthermore, a number of countries still maintain restrictions on the export, import, and/or use of encryption. Patents and licensing issues may affect which commercial encryption schemes can be used. Common factors that influence the choice of encryption algorithm are as follows:

■ Required security

  ■ Value of the data (to either the organization and/or other entities—the more valuable the data, the stronger the required encryption)

---

[56] For more information about AES, see http://csrc.nist.gov/publications/fips/fips197/fips-197.pdf.

[57] Triple DES is considerably slower than AES. For more information about DES and 3DES, see http://csrc.ncsl.nist.gov/cryptval/.

[58] For more information about the SHA and the associated Secure Hash Standard (SHS), see FIPS PUB 180-2, *Secure Hash Standard*, http://csrc.nist.gov/publications/fips/fips180-2/fips180-2withchangenotice.pdf. NIST has recommended that the use of SHA-1 be phased out by 2010 in favor of SHA-224, SHA-256, and other larger, stronger hash functions. See http://csrc.nist.gov/hash_standards_comments.pdf for additional information.

[59] AES 128 is the exception to this rule because it provides higher performance and security than 3DES.

- Time value of data (if data is valuable but for only a short time period [e.g., days as opposed to years], then a weaker encryption algorithm could be used)

- Threat to data (the higher the threat level, the stronger the required encryption)

- Other protective measures that are in place and that may reduce the need for stronger encryption—for example, using protected methods of communications, such as dedicated circuits as opposed to the public Internet

- Required performance (higher performance requirements may require procurement of additional system resources, such as a hardware cryptographic accelerator, or may necessitate weaker encryption)

- System resources (fewer resources [e.g., process, memory] may necessitate weaker encryption)

- Import, export, or usage restrictions

- Encryption schemes supported by Web server application

- Encryption schemes supported by Web browsers of expected users.

7.5.5 Implementing SSL/TLS

A digital signature is needed to implement SSL/TLS on a Web server. A certificate, which is the digital equivalent of an ID card, is used in conjunction with a public key encryption system. Certificates can be issued by trusted third parties, known as CAs, or can be self-signed. Organizational requirements determine which approach is used.

Although the sequence of steps is not identical for all Web servers, the implementation of a third-party signed certificate for a Web server generally includes at least three steps:

- Generating and submitting a certificate-signing request (CSR)

- Picking up a signed SSL/TLS certificate from a CA

- Installing the certificate and configuring the Web server to use SSL/TLS for any specified resources.

A CSR consists of three parts: certification request information, a signature algorithm identifier, and a digital signature over the certification request information. Web servers that are SSL/TLS enabled provide specific instructions for the generation of a CSR. There are two major types of CSRs. The most popular is the encoded Public Key Cryptography Standard (PKCS) #10, Certification Request Syntax Standard, which is used by newer Web servers [RSA00]. The other CSR type, based on the Privacy Enhanced Mail (PEM) specification, is called either PEM message header or Web site professional format. The use of this CSR is generally limited to older Web servers. Most Web servers generate PKCS #10-compliant CSRs similar to the sample CSR shown in Figure 7-2. A CSR provides not only additional information about a given entity, or a "challenge password" by which the entity may later request certificate revocation, but also attributes for inclusion in X.509 certificates [RSA00].

```
-----BEGIN CERTIFICATE REQUEST-----
MIIBujCCASMCAQAwejELMAkGA1UEBhMCQ0ExEzARBgNVBAgTClRFc3QgU3RhdGUx
ETAPBgNVBAcTCENvbG9yYWR0MRswGQYDVQQKExJDYW5hZGlhbiBUZXN0IE9yZy4x
EjAQBgNVBAsTCU9VIE9mZmljZTESMBAGA1UEAxMJd3d3LmV4LmNhMIGfMA0GCSqG
SIb3DQEBAQUAA4GNADCBiQKBgQD5PIij2FNa+Zfk1OHtptspcSBkfkfZ3jFxYA6ypo3+YbQ
hO3PLTvNfQj9mhb0xWyvoNvL8Gnp1GUPgiw9GvRao603yHebgc2bioAKoTkWTmW+C8+Ka
42wMVrgcW32rNYmDnDWOSBWWR1L1j1YkQBK1nQnQzV3U/h0mr+ASE/nV7wIDAQABo
AAwDQYJKoZIhvcNAQEEBQADgYEAAAhxY1dcw6P8cDEDG4UiwB0DOoQnFb3WYV17d4
+6lfOtKfuL/Ep0blLWXQoVpOICF3gfAF6wcAbeg5MtiWwTwvXRtJ2jszsZbpOuIt0WU1+cCYi
vxuTil8CQNQrsrD4s2ZJytkzDTAcz1Nmiuh93eqYw+kydUyRYlOMEIomNFIQ=
-----END CERTIFICATE REQUEST-----
```

Figure 7-2. Sample CSR

Spelling and punctuation should be checked when information is provided during the CSR generation process. The URL that is supplied must exactly match the URL for which the certificate is used. SSL/TLS clients are configured to generate an error if the URLs do not match. In some instances, a user may acknowledge this error in an alert box and proceed.

Once the CSR has been generated, the organization submits it to a CA. The CA's role is to fulfill the CSR by authenticating the requesting entity and verifying the entity's signature. If the request is valid, the CA constructs an X.509 certificate from the domain name (DN) and public key; the issuer name (more commonly referred to as the common name [CN]); and the CA's choice of serial number, validity period, or signature algorithm. Upon receiving a submitted CSR, the CA must verify the CSR and create a signed X.509 certificate. At this point, most CAs will then alert the applicant by telephone, e-mail, etc., that the X.509 certificate is available. Once notified, applicants will be able to download their certificates through an SSL/TLS-protected Web-based interface.

Figure 7-3 shows an X.509 certificate encoded in PEM format. Similar to the CSR, when supplying a certificate to a configuration wizard or even saving it to a hard drive, the lines "BEGIN CERTIFICATE" and "END CERTIFICATE" are vital. Without them, the Web server application will be unable to interpret the encoded contents of the certificate.

```
-----BEGIN CERTIFICATE-----
MIIDjjCCAvegAwIBAgIBAzANBgkqhkiG9w0BAQQFADCBzzELMAkGA1UEBhMCQ0ExED
AOBgNVBAgTB09udGFyaW8xETAPBgNVBAcTCFdhdGVybG9vMR8wHQYDVQQKExZVb
ml2ZXJzaXR5IG9mIFdhdGVybG9vMSswKQYDVQQLEyJJbmZvcm1hdGlvbiBTeXN0ZW1zI
GFuZCBUZWNobm9sb2d5MSUwIwYDVQQDExxVVy9JU1QgQ2VydGlmaWNhdGUgQXV0a
G9yaXR5MSYwJAYJKoZIhvcNAQkBFhdpc3QtY2FaaXN0LnV3YXRlcmxvby5jYTAeFw05O
DA4MjcxNjE0NDZaFw05OTEwMjExNjE0NDZaMIHGMQswCQYDVQQGEwJDQTEQMA4G
A1UECBMHT250YXJpbzERMA8GA1UEBxMIV2F0ZXJsb28xHzAdBgNVBAoTFlVuaXZlcn
NpdHkgb2YgV2F0ZXJsb28xKzApBgNVBAsTIkluZm9ybWF0aW9uIFN5c3RlbXMgYW5kIFRl
Y2hub2xvZ3kxGTAXBgNVBAMTEGlzdC51d2F0ZXJsb28uY2ExKTAnBgkqhkiG9w0BCQEW
GndlYm1hc3RlckBpc3QudXdhdGVybG9vLmNhMIGfMA0GCSqGSIb3DQEBAQUAA4GNAD
CBiQKBgQCw8Sc7X4EeAxBxTPgmTd4Utau0BIqYTdnIRXXg/ryAn2A7G5MtkMHj0triXoineu
RxW9MQSQW8jMAv+xznMaL6OxnG+txyBjYx1zh02D+npBp4Fy81kgbypp5Usf18BonsqSe9Sl
2P0opCCyclGr+i4agSP5RM5KrycTSVoKHERQIDAQABo4GAMH4wOgYJYIZIAYb4QgEEB
C0WK2h0dHA6Ly9pc3QudXdhdGVybG9vLmNhL3NlY3VyaXR5L2NhLWNybC5zZW0wLQ
YJYIZIAYb4QgENBCAWHklzc3VpbmcgQ0EgYXNzdW1lcyBubyBsaWFibGl0eTARBglghkgB
hvhCAQEEBAMCAEAwDQYJKoZIhvcNAQEEBQADgYEADZOtbpvbnBaWOPIMOSbqTQK
1LUjn4uHN3BLmqxznIzdiMu4RXyxne5Uq9EA7LbttutH7fIoOW+ID9Zrn1aH1FoU1dtEvovXm
A6m5G+SN8A9tIAvRGjNmphB82xGkwEXuLN0afYz5XaFo3Z73INw6WxVoxDhPTgNIyYEii
Sp6Qfc=
-----END CERTIFICATE-----
```

Figure 7-3. Sample Encoded SSL/TLS Certificate

When a Web browser contacts a Web site that is using SSL/TLS, the browser examines the certificate and attempts to verify its validity. Each browser has a store of certificates, and these typically include root certificates for many third-party CAs. If the browser has a root certificate for the third-party CA that issued the Web server's certificate, it can use the CA's root certificate to validate the Web server's certificate, which is based partially on that root certificate. If the browser does not have the needed root certificate, then it typically displays a warning to the user that says the Web server's certificate could not be verified and asks the user how it should proceed.

Some organizations decide to create and sign their own Web server certificates instead of having certificates issued by third-party CAs. The main advantage of self-signed certificates is that it avoids the cost of purchasing and renewing certificates; however, by default, Web browsers will not be able to validate self-signed certificates, so they provide no assurance of the legitimacy of the certificate or the Web server. Given the increasing use of phishing and other techniques to trick users into visiting rogue Web sites, failing to authenticate the server's identity before using SSL/TLS with it is unacceptable. If a particular Web server is only going to be accessed from the organization's own systems (e.g., telecommuters using laptops issued and managed by the organization), then those systems' browsers could be provisioned with the root certificates needed to validate the Web server's self-signed certificate and authenticate the server's identity. Otherwise, the use of self-signed certificates for public Web servers is generally not recommended because of the logistics involved in securely distributing the root certificates to users' Web browsers and having the certificates installed correctly by the users so that the browsers can authenticate the organization's Web servers.

For all SSL/TLS certificates for Web servers, regardless of issuer or format, administrators should take extreme caution in securing their certificate and encryption keys. The following are recommendations:

- Create and store a backup copy of the certificate on read-only media in case the original certificate is deleted accidentally. If the certificate is lost and cannot be recovered from backup media, a new certificate must be created.

■ Create and store a backup copy of the encryption keys on read-only media in case the keys are deleted accidentally. If the keys are lost and cannot be recovered from backup media, a new key pair and certificate must be created. Note that the backup copy of the keys must be physically secured and should be encrypted as well.

■ Store the original certificate in a folder or partition accessible by only Web or system administrators and secured by appropriate authentication mechanisms.

■ Consider running a file integrity checker in the Web server (see Section 8.2.2) and ensure that it is monitoring for any changes to the certificate.

■ Examine system logs regularly to validate and ensure prevention of unauthorized system access.

If a malicious user gains unauthorized access to a Web server, the integrity of the entire server is lost immediately once the encryption key pair is modified. Once a key in an SSL/TLS certificate is compromised, it can remain compromised; for example, some CAs do not issue revocation information, and many client implementations do not obtain or process revocation information.

Once a certificate is ready, it needs to be installed, and SSL needs to be enabled and configured. Some steps are common to all Web servers:

■ Disable SSL 1.0 and SSL 2.0.

■ Configure SSL/TLS to restrict cryptographic algorithms to the selected cipher suite(s) (see Section 7.5.4).

■ Indicate the location of the SSL/TLS certificate and instruct the server to start using SSL/TLS. In certain cases, the Web server must be instructed to begin using SSL/TLS, and even given the location of the SSL/TLS certificate and private keys if they were stored as files on the hard drive.

■ Instruct server to listen on TCP port 443. This is the default TCP port from which SSL/TLS resources are accessed by clients (other ports can be used). In most cases, if the server was not previously using SSL/TLS, this port would be disabled for security reasons. It will probably be necessary to configure the network infrastructure supporting the Web server to allow SSL/TLS traffic (see Section 8.2). All ports other than TCP 443 should be closed and the network infrastructure (e.g., firewalls) should be updated to block attempts to connect to all other ports. However, if the Web server is to host both HTTP and HTTPS content, TCP 80 should be open as well.

■ Configure the server to protect the necessary resources (directories and/or files) using SSL/TLS. Configure the Web server application so that the appropriate resources are protected with SSL/TLS. These resources are then accessible only from a URL that starts with "https://".

Newer versions of the HTML standard have been amended to include a response to inform clients when a file they have requested is available only via SSL/TLS. The HTTP status code 403.4 indicates that a HTTP GET request must be prefixed with an https:// because the resource requested is protected with SSL/TLS. For more information, consult RFCs 2246, 2626, and 2817.[60] Most current Web browsers also provide users with some user-friendly visual indication of a server's SSL/TLS certificate status, such as changing the color of a status bar.

---

[60] http://www.ietf.org/rfc/rfc2246.txt, http://www.ietf.org/rfc/rfc2626.txt and http://www.ietf.org/rfc/rfc2817.txt

7.5.6 SSL/TLS Implementations

Although some Web servers come packaged with SSL capabilities already integrated, many do not. This section discusses various commercial and open-source SSL/TLS implementations. Some of these packages contain the functionality to generate SSL certificates without the need of a CA. The following list includes some of the SSL toolkits available:

- OpenSSL is an open-source implementation of SSL/TLS for Unix and Linux platforms (http://www.openssl.org/).

- Network Security Services (NSS) is an open-source implementation of SSL/TLS developed by the Mozilla foundation.[61] NSS is derived from the original Netscape SSL implementation.

- GnuTLS is an open-source implementation of SSL/TLS developed by the Free Software Foundation.[62]

- Java Secure Socket Extension (JSSE) is an implementation of SSL/TLS developed by Sun for distribution as part of the Java Runtime Environment (JRE).[63]

- Security Support Provider Interface (SSPI) is an implementation of SSL/TLS available on Microsoft Windows Server 2003.

- IBM Java Secure Sockets Extension (IBMJSSE) is an implementation of SSL/TLS for the WebSphere Application Server.

Federal government organizations are required to use Federal Information Processing Standards (FIPS)-validated SSL/TLS implementations when protecting data using SSL/TLS. The Cryptographic Module Validation Program (CMVP) performs validation testing of cryptographic modules, including SSL/TLS implementations.[64] NIST provides a list of FIPS 140-2[65]-compliant vendors and implementations.[66] Regardless of what SSL/TLS implementation is used, it is important to ensure that security patches are regularly applied. Security flaws in SSL/TLS implementations can potentially allow attackers to spoof PKI certificates, forge digital signatures, perform DoS attacks, or execute arbitrary code in the Web server.

7.6 Brute Force Attacks

Many Web sites authenticate users via username and password combinations—whether through HTTP Basic, HTTP Digest, or a Web form over SSL. Regardless of implementation, username and password combinations are susceptible to brute force attacks. Brute force attacks can occur in multiple forms:

- **Username Harvesting**—Applications that differentiate between an invalid password and an invalid username can allow attackers to construct a list of valid user accounts.

---

[61] http://www.mozilla.org/projects/security/pki/nss/
[62] http://www.gnu.org/software/gnutls/
[63] http://java.sun.com/products/jsse/index.jsp
[64] http://csrc.nist.gov/cryptval/
[65] http://csrc.nist.gov/publications/fips/fips140-2/fips1402.pdf
[66] http://csrc.nist.gov/cryptval/140-1/1401vend.htm

- **Dictionary Attacks**—Attackers use common dictionary words and their variants to attempt to gain access to a user's account.

- **Brute Force Attacks**—Attackers try every possible password to attempt to gain access to a user's account.

There are a number of methods for reducing a Web server's vulnerability to brute force attack:

- **Use Strong Authentication**—Strong authentication techniques, such as hardware tokens, one-time passwords, biometric authentication, and SSL/TLS client certificates, are much more resistant to brute force attacks than passwords. Stronger authentication can be achieved by combining multiple authentication mechanisms to form a multi-factor authentication scheme. However, strong authentication may be prohibitively expensive or difficult to incorporate into a system.

- **Use Timeouts**—Incurring a delay of several seconds after a failed login attempt can slow an attacker down. However, attackers can attempt multiple logins at the same time from different clients.

- **Use Lockouts**—Locking out a user account after a number of failed login attempts prevents the attacker from successfully logging into an account. The primary disadvantage of this technique is that it can leave the system open to a DoS attack. Also, an attacker may try several common passwords against random usernames, which may grant the attacker access to the system while bypassing the lockout [Whit06].

- **Enforce a Password Policy**—By requiring passwords to be of a certain length and to contain lowercase letters, uppercase letters, numerals, and/or symbols, a simple dictionary attack will not work on the system.

- **Enforce a Password Change Policy**—By requiring passwords to be changed on a regular basis, an attacker might not have enough time to brute-force a potential password. However, strict password change policies can frustrate users and weaken passwords by causing users to follow patterns, such as using password1, password2, etc. [Bell06]

- **Use Blacklists**—Blocking IP addresses or domains known to attempt brute force attacks from accessing the system may stop some attackers, but it is possible that some attacks may come from compromised systems that would otherwise be considered legitimate.

- **Use Log Monitoring Software**—Vigilantly monitoring logs of invalid password attempts may help an organization detect brute force attacks, potentially giving the organization time to respond before the attack has been successful.

Aside from strong authentication, none of these mechanisms completely prevent brute force attacks; however, using one or more of these techniques makes it more difficult for an attacker to gain access to the system. Nevertheless, when considering which technologies to adopt, it is important to consider passwords as part of the system as a whole. For example, a Web site that uses usernames and passwords to retrieve user customizations may not need to concern itself with preventing brute force attacks [Bell06]. In systems where sensitive information is being protected, some of these techniques may be necessary. Regardless, an organization may already have policies regarding brute force attacks. If so, those policies should be followed and enhanced if necessary.

7.7 Checklist for Using Authentication and Encryption Technologies for Web Servers

Completed	Action
	Configure Web authentication and encryption technologies
☐	For Web resources that require minimal protection and for which there is a small, clearly defined audience, configure address-based authentication
☐	For Web resources that require additional protection but for which there is a small, clearly defined audience, configure address-based authentication as a second line of defense
☐	For Web resources that require minimal protection but for which there is no clearly defined audience, configure basic or digest authentication (better)
☐	For Web resources that require protection from malicious bots, configure basic or digest authentication (better) or implement mitigation techniques discussed in Section 5.2.4
☐	For organizations required to comply with FIPS 140-2, ensure the SSL/TLS implementation is FIPS-validated
☐	For Web resources that require maximum protection, configure SSL/TLS
	Configure SSL/TLS
☐	Ensure the SSL/TLS implementation is fully patched
☐	Use a third-party issued certificate for server authentication (unless all systems using the server are organization-managed, in which case a self-signed certificate could potentially be used instead)
☐	For configurations that require a medium level of client authentication, configure server to require username and password via SSL/TLS
☐	For configurations that require a high level of client authentication, configure server to require client certificates via SSL/TLS
☐	Ensure weak cipher suites are disabled (see Table 7.1 for the recommended usage of Federal cipher suites)
☐	Configure file integrity checker to monitor Web server certificate
☐	If only SSL/TLS is to be used in the Web server, ensure access via any TCP port other than 443 is disabled
☐	If most traffic to the Web server will be via encrypted SSL/TLS, ensure that appropriate logging and detection mechanisms are employed in the Web server (because network monitoring is ineffective against encrypted SSL/TLS sessions)
	Protect against brute force attacks
☐	Use strong authentication if possible
☐	Use a delay after failed login attempts
☐	Lock out an account after a set number of failed login attempts
☐	Enforce a password policy
☐	Blacklist IP addresses or domains known to attempt brute force attacks
☐	Use log monitoring software to detect brute force attacks

8.   Implementing a Secure Network Infrastructure

The network infrastructure that supports the Web server plays a critical role in the security of the Web server. In most configurations, the network infrastructure is the first line of defense between the Internet and a public Web server. Network design alone, however, cannot protect a Web server. The frequency, sophistication, and variety of attacks perpetrated today lend support to the idea that Web security must be implemented through layered and diverse protection mechanisms (defense-in-depth). This section discusses those network components that can support and protect Web servers to further enhance their overall security. Although security issues are paramount, network infrastructure considerations are influenced by many factors other than security, including cost, performance, and reliability.

8.1   Network Composition and Structure

Firewalls and routers are devices or systems that control the flow of network traffic between networks. They can protect Web servers from vulnerabilities inherent in the TCP/IP suite and help reduce the security issues associated with insecure applications and OSs. However, an organization has many choices when determining a network environment for a Web server, and security may not be the principal factor in deciding among those options. Network composition and structure are the first and in many respects the most critical decisions that affect Web server security because they determine what network infrastructure elements protect the Web server. For example, if the Web server is located before the organization's main firewall, then the firewall cannot be used to control traffic to and from the Web server. Network composition and structure also determine what other portions of the network are vulnerable if the Web server is compromised. For example, an externally accessible Web server located on the internal production network subjects the internal network to attack if the Web server is compromised. Also, an organization may choose not to have the Web server located on its network at all and to outsource the hosting to a third party.

8.1.1   Inadvisable Network Layout

Some organizations choose to locate their public Web servers on their internal production networks. That is, their Web servers reside on the same network as the internal users and servers. The principal weakness of this layout is that it exposes internal network components to additional risks. Web servers are often targets of attackers. If attackers manage to compromise a Web server, they will have access to the internal network and will be able to more easily compromise internal hosts. Therefore, this layout is not recommended.

Another network layout that is not generally recommended is placing the Web server before an organization's firewall or router that provides IP filtering. In this structure, the network provides little, if any, protection for the Web server. Because the Web server itself has to maintain security, it provides a single point of failure. To be even somewhat secure in this location, the Web server OS and application have to be extremely well-hardened, with all unnecessary and insecure services disabled and all necessary security patches applied. To maintain the security of the setup, the Web server administrator must stay up to date on vulnerabilities and related patches. Another limitation of this structure is that providing any sort of secure remote administration or content update capability is difficult.

8.1.2   Demilitarized Zone

A demilitarized zone (DMZ) describes a host or network segment inserted as a "neutral zone" between an organization's private network and the Internet. It prevents outside users of the Web server from gaining direct access to an organization's internal network (intranet). A DMZ mitigates the risks of locating a Web server on an internal network or exposing it directly to the Internet. It is a compromise solution that offers the most benefits with the least amount of risk for most organizations. The DMZ allows access to the resources located within it to both internal and external users. There are a wide variety of DMZ configurations, each with its own strengths and weaknesses.

Creating a DMZ involves placing a firewall between an organization's border router and its internal network, and creating a new network segment that can only be reached through the DMZ device. The Web server is placed on the new segment, along with other network infrastructure components and servers that need to be externally accessible. In some configurations, the border router itself may act as a basic firewall. Figure 8-1 illustrates an example of this simple DMZ using a router with access control lists (ACL) to restrict certain types of network traffic to and from the DMZ.

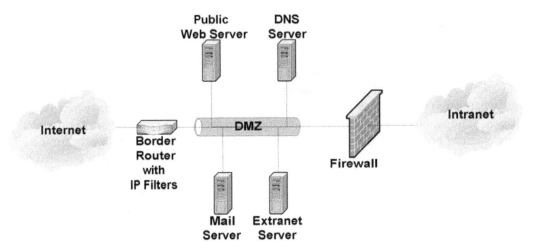

Figure 8-1. Simple Single-Firewall DMZ

A single-firewall DMZ is a low-cost approach because the organization needs only to add a single firewall and use its existing border router to provide protection to the DMZ. It is usually appropriate only for small organizations that face a minimal threat. The basic weakness in the approach is that although the router is able to protect against most network attacks, it is not "aware" of the Web server application layer protocols (e.g., HTTP) and thus cannot protect against application layer attacks aimed at the Web server. A superior approach is to add a second firewall between the Internet and the DMZ, as shown in Figure 8-2.

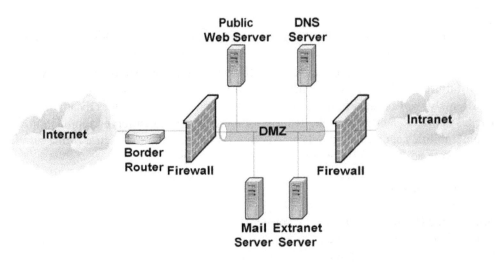

Figure 8-2. Two-Firewall DMZ

A two-firewall DMZ configuration improves protection over a router-firewall DMZ because the dedicated firewalls can have more complex and powerful security rule sets. In addition, because a dedicated firewall is often able to analyze incoming and outgoing HTTP traffic, it can detect and defend against application layer attacks aimed at the Web server. Depending on the rule sets of the firewalls and the level of traffic the DMZ receives, this type of DMZ may result in some performance degradation.

For organizations that desire the security of the two-firewall DMZ but do not have the resources to purchase two firewalls, another option exists called the "service leg" DMZ. In this configuration, a firewall is constructed with three (or more) network interfaces. One network interface attaches to the border router, another interface attaches to the internal network, and a third network interface connects to the DMZ (see Figure 8-3).

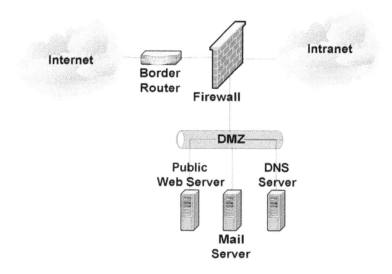

Figure 8-3. Service Leg DMZ

This configuration subjects the firewall to an increased risk of service degradation during a DoS attack aimed at the DMZ. In the standard single-firewall DMZ network configuration discussed above, a DoS attack against the Web server generally affects only the Web server. In a service-leg DMZ network configuration, the firewall bears the brunt of any DoS attack because it must examine any network traffic before the traffic reaches the Web server (or any other DMZ or internal network resource) [NIST02a]. However, it is increasingly likely that a DoS attack will take the form of a DDoS attack and consume all of the incoming network bandwidth and related devices (e.g., Internet border routers) before ever reaching a DMZ firewall.

The advantages of a DMZ from a security standpoint are as follows:

■ The Web server may be better protected, and network traffic to and from the Web server can be monitored.

■ Compromise of the Web server does not directly threaten the internal production network.

■ Greater control can be provided over the security of the Web server because traffic to and from the Web server can be controlled.

■ The DMZ network configuration can be optimized to support and protect the Web servers.

8-3

The disadvantages of a DMZ from a security standpoint are as follows:

■ DoS attacks aimed at the Web server may have an effect on the internal network.

■ Depending on the firewall configuration controlling traffic between the DMZ and internal network, it may be possible for the Web server to be used to attack or compromise hosts on the internal network. In other words, protection offered by the DMZ depends in large part on the firewall configuration.

For organizations that support their own Web server, a DMZ is almost invariably the best option. It offers protection for the Web server and other externally accessible servers without exposing the internal network. However, it should only be considered secure when employed in conjunction with the other steps discussed in this document.

8.1.3 Outsourced Hosting

Some organizations choose to outsource the hosting of their Web servers to a third party (e.g., an ISP, Web hosting service, or other government agency). In this case, the Web server would not be located on the organization's network. The hosting service network would have a dedicated network that hosts many Web servers (for many organizations) operating on a single network (see Figure 8-4).

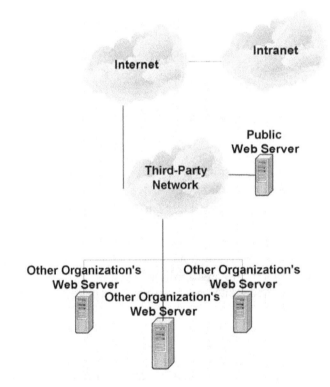

Figure 8-4. Outsourced Web Server Hosting

From a security standpoint, the advantages of outsourcing are as follows:

■ DoS attacks aimed at the Web server have no effect on the organization's production network.

■ Compromise of the Web server does not directly threaten the internal production network.

■ The outsourcer may have greater knowledge of securing and protecting Web servers.

■ The network can be optimized solely for the support and protection of Web servers.

The disadvantages of outsourcing from a security standpoint are as follows:

■ It requires trusting a third party with Web server content.

■ It is more difficult to remotely administer the Web server or remotely update Web server content.

■ Less control can be provided over the security of the Web server.

■ The Web server may be affected by attacks aimed at other Web servers hosted by the outsourcer on the same network.

Outsourcing often makes sense for smaller organizations that cannot afford to support the necessary Web server staff. It may also be appropriate for larger organizations that do not wish to host their own Web servers. Outsourcing usually does not make sense for organizations that wish to maintain tight control over their Web servers.

8.1.4 Management Network

Web servers and other important components can be connected to each other and managed through an organization's standard networks or through a separate network known as a management network. If a management network is used, each host being managed through the network has an additional network interface known as a management interface that connects to the management network. Also, each host being managed is unable to pass any traffic between its management interface and any of its other network interfaces. Consoles and other hosts that are used to manage the Web components are attached to the management network only. This architecture effectively isolates the management network from the production networks. The benefits of doing this are to protect the components from some attacks and to ensure that the components can be managed under adverse conditions (e.g., DDoS attack). Disadvantages of using a management network include the additional costs of networking equipment and other hardware (e.g., personal computers [PC] for the consoles) and the inconvenience for Web component administrators of using separate computers for management and monitoring.

8.2 Network Element Configuration

Once the Web server has been positioned in the network, the network infrastructure elements should be configured to support and protect it. The primary elements of a network infrastructure that affect Web server security are firewalls, routers, IDSs, intrusion prevention systems (IPS), switches, load balancers, and reverse proxies. Each has an important role to play and is critical to the overall strategy of protecting the Web server through defense-in-depth. Unfortunately, when it comes to securing a Web server, there is no single "silver bullet" solution. A firewall or IPS alone cannot adequately protect a public Web server from all threats or attacks.

8.2.1 Router/Firewall Configuration

Several types of firewalls exist. The most basic firewalls are routers that can provide access control for IP packets. In the middle are stateful firewalls that can provide access control based on TCP and User

Datagram Protocol (UDP) as well as IP. The most powerful firewalls are application layer or proxy firewalls that are able to understand and filter Web content.[67]

A common misperception about firewalls (and routers acting as firewalls) is that they eliminate all risk and can protect against misconfiguration of the Web server or poor network design. Unfortunately, this is not the case. Firewalls and routers themselves are vulnerable to misconfiguration and software vulnerabilities. In addition, many firewalls have limited insight into the application layer where many attacks occur. Thus, Web servers in particular are vulnerable to many attacks, even when located behind a secure, well-configured firewall.

A firewall (or router acting as a firewall) that is protecting a Web server should be configured to block all access to the Web server from the Internet except the necessary ports, such as TCP ports 80 (HTTP) and 443 (HTTPS). A firewall is the first line of defense for a Web server; however, to be truly secure, organizations need to implement layered protection for their Web servers (and networks). Most importantly, organizations should strive to maintain all systems in a secure posture and not depend solely on firewalls, routers, or any other single component to stop attackers.

A modern enterprise router is able to function as a network and transport layer filter (e.g., a basic firewall). A router functioning as a network/transport layer firewall can provide filtering based on several pieces of information [NIST02a], including the following:

- Source IP address

- Destination IP address

- Traffic type

- TCP/UDP port number and state.

The strength of routers is in their cost. Most organizations already have a border router that can be configured to provide network/transport layer firewall capabilities.

The weaknesses of routers include the following:

- Susceptibility to application layer attacks (e.g., cannot examine Web content for embedded malicious code)

- Susceptibility to attacks via allowed ports

- Difficulty of configuration and administration

- Limitations in logging capabilities

- Processing capabilities that may be more limited and overtaxed by complex rule sets (i.e., access control lists)

- Insufficient rule set expressiveness and filtering capabilities.

---

[67] For more information about firewalls, see NIST SP 800-41, *Guidelines on Firewalls and Firewall Policy* (http://csrc.nist.gov/publications/nistpubs/).

The only "pure" network layer firewalls available today are small office/home office (SOHO) firewall appliances and personal firewalls [NIST02a] that may only perform basic packet-level filtering.

Stateful inspection firewalls are transport layer devices that incorporate "awareness" of the state of a TCP connection. Stateful inspection firewalls maintain internal information, such as the state of the connections passing through them and the contents of some of the data streams. This allows better and more accurate rule sets and filtering to be specified. Stateful inspection firewalls add the capability to enforce rules based on connection state to the capabilities of a filtering router.

Application layer firewalls (sometimes called application-proxy gateway firewalls) are advanced firewalls that combine network and transport layer access control with application layer functionality. Application layer firewalls permit no traffic directly between the Internet and the internal network. They can usually perform extensive logging and access control.

Application layer firewalls are considered the most secure type of firewall and have numerous advantages over packet filtering routers and stateful inspection firewalls, including the following:

- Logging capabilities

- Filtering capabilities (can filter specific types of Web content and specific HTTP commands)

- Protocol conformance

- Validation of protocol behaviors

- Integrated signature-based detection of application layer attacks

- Ease of configuration

- User authentication capabilities.

The primary disadvantages that application layer firewalls have when compared to packet filtering routers and stateful inspection firewalls are as follows:

- Speed of throughput (if platform is not adequately sized)

- Cost (if high-end hardware is required to operate efficiently)

- Inadequate support for less popular and new protocols.

Although not strictly a limitation, some application layer firewalls are implemented on hosts running general-purpose OSs (e.g., Windows, Linux, Unix). This arrangement introduces an added layer of complexity and some additional risk because the general-purpose OS must also be secured in addition to the firewall software itself. Application layer firewalls are increasingly being deployed as appliance-based devices, which may use specialized OSs. Routers and stateful inspection firewalls also typically run on specialized OSs.

To successfully protect a Web server using a firewall, ensure that the firewall is patched to the latest or most secure level (both the application and the underlying OS) and is configured to perform the following:

- Control all traffic between the Internet and the Web server

■ Block all inbound traffic to the Web server except traffic which is required, such as TCP ports 80 (HTTP) and/or 443 (HTTPS)

■ Block all inbound traffic with an internal IP address (to prevent IP spoofing attacks)

■ Block client connections from the Web server to the Internet and the organization's internal network (this will reduce the impact of some successful compromises)

■ Block (in conjunction with the intrusion detection or prevention system [see Section 8.2.2]) IP addresses or subnets that the IDS or IPS reports are attacking the organizational network

■ Notify the network or Web server administrator or appropriate security personnel of suspicious activity through an appropriate means (e.g., page, e-mail, network trap)

■ Provide content filtering

■ Protect against DoS attacks

■ Detect malformed or known attack URL requests

■ Log critical events, including the following details:

   ■ Time/date

   ■ Interface IP address

   ■ Manufacturer-specific event name

   ■ Standard attack event (if one exists)

   ■ Source and destination IP addresses

   ■ Source and destination port numbers

   ■ Network protocol.

Most firewalls perform some type of logging of the traffic they receive. For most firewalls, the default logging configuration is suitable, provided logging is enabled. Administrators should consult the manufacturer's documentation if they believe they require additional information to be logged. Certain firewalls include an ability to track and log information for each rule, which enables accountability to a very specific extent.

Many firewalls support the ability to selectively decide what information to log. If a firewall receives a series of similar packets from the same location, it may decide not to log any additional packets after the first one. Although this is a valuable feature, consider the consequences: each packet that is dropped and not logged is potential evidence of malicious intent. The principle of logging, a fundamental aspect of accountability, is discussed in detail in Section 9.1.

As with OSs and other security-enforcing elements, a firewall requires updates. This includes updating firmware for hardware and router-based firewalls. Specific instructions on how to update a firewall are found in the manufacturer's documentation. Administrators should check for firewall updates frequently.

8.2.2 Intrusion Detection and Prevention Systems

An IDS is an application that monitors the events occurring in a system or network and analyzes them for signs of potential incidents, which are violations or imminent threats of violation of computer security policies, acceptable use policies, or standard security practices.[68] An IPS has all the capabilities of an IDS and can also attempt to stop potential incidents. Because IDS and IPS systems offer many of the same capabilities, they are often collectively called intrusion detection and prevention systems (IDPS). When an IDPS detects a potential incident, it notifies administrators through IDPS console messages, emails, pages, or other mechanisms.

The two types of IDPSs most relevant for Web security are host-based and network-based.[69] A host-based IDPS monitors the characteristics of a single host and the events occurring within that host to identify and stop suspicious activity. Host-based IDPS software must be installed on each individual computer that is to be monitored or protected. Host-based IDPSs are very closely integrated with the OSs of the host computers they protect. Thus, a host-based IDPS must be designed specifically for each OS (and often each version of that OS). Host-based IDPSs monitor various aspects of hosts, such as network traffic, system logs, running processes, file access and modification, and system and application configuration changes.

Host-based IDPSs are especially useful when most of the network traffic to and from a Web server is encrypted (e.g., SSL/TLS is in use) because the functionality and capability of network-based IDPSs (see below) is severely limited when network traffic is encrypted. Also, because they are located on the server, host-based IDPSs can detect some attacks and penetration attempts not recognized by network-based IDPSs. Unfortunately, host-based IDPSs can have a negative effect on host performance. In general, enabling more extensive detection capabilities and having more events to monitor both have a negative impact on the performance of the host. Host-based IDPSs may not detect some network-based attacks, such as certain DoS attacks. If a host-based IDPS is on a Web server that is compromised, it is very likely that the attacker will also compromise the IDPS itself.

A network-based IDPS monitors network traffic for particular network segments or network devices and analyzes the network and application protocol activity to identify and stop suspicious activity. Most network-based IDPSs use predefined "attack signatures" to detect and identify attacks. Attack signatures are patterns that correspond to known types of intrusions. Network-based IDPSs also use other detection methods to identify anomalous activity, protocol violations, and other unusual activity.

Unlike a host-based IDPS, a network-based IDPS can monitor network activity for many hosts simultaneously. Network-based IDPSs can usually detect more network-based attacks and can more easily provide a comprehensive picture of the current attacks against a network. Because network-based IDPSs are installed on dedicated hosts, they do not have a negative effect on the performance of the Web server host and are not immediately compromised by a successful attack on the Web server.

Network-based IDPSs do have some limitations. The timing of an attack can have a significant impact on the ability of a network-based IDPS to detect an attack. For example, if an attacker spreads out the timing of an attack over a period of hours or days, the attack may not be detected by the IDPS. Network configuration, such as the use of asymmetric routing, can have a negative impact on the ability of a

---

[68] For more information about IDPSs, see NIST SP 800-94, *Guide to Intrusion Detection and Prevention Systems (IDPS)* (http://csrc.nist.gov/publications/nistpubs/).

[69] Other major IDPS categories include wireless IDPS, which examines wireless networking protocols only, and network behavior anomaly detection software, which monitors network traffic flows for flow anomalies. Neither of these types of IDPS technologies analyzes Web activity.

network-based IDPS to detect attacks. Network-based IDPSs are also more susceptible to being disabled by DoS attacks (even those not directly targeted at the IDPS). Also, depending on how the network-based IDPS is integrated into the network, it is possible to negatively affect the availability of the network in the event of an IDPS hardware failure.

Both host-based and network-based IDPSs require frequent updates to their attack signature databases so that they can recognize new attacks. An IDPS that is not updated frequently will fail to recognize the latest (and often most popular) attacks. Both types of IDPSs may be limited in their ability to detect zero-day attacks because it is unlikely that an appropriate signature is available. A host-based IDPS may have a better chance of detecting a zero-day attack because it is better able to detect the actions taken by an attacker after a successful exploit (e.g., new unauthorized privileged accounts, installation of malicious software).

File integrity checkers are a simple form of host-based IDPS. A file integrity checker computes and stores a hash for every file of interest and establishes a database of file hashes. It provides a tool for system administrators to recognize changes to files, particularly unauthorized changes. File integrity checkers are available as standalone products and bundled with other host-based IDPS techniques. Some host-based IDPSs can monitor file access attempts and stop suspicious attempts to read, modify, delete, and execute files. A host-based IDPS with this capability could be configured to protect important Web server files.

To successfully protect a Web server using an IDPS, ensure that the IDPS is configured to—

■ Monitor network traffic to and from the Web server

■ Monitor changes to critical files on the Web server (file integrity checking capability)[70]

■ Monitor the system resources available on the Web server host (host-based)

■ Block (in conjunction with the firewall) IP addresses or subnets that are attacking the organizational network

■ Notify the appropriate parties (e.g., IDPS administrator, Web server administrator, incident response team) of suspected attacks through appropriate means according to the organizational incident response policy and procedures

■ Detect as wide a variety of scanning and attacks as possible with an acceptable level of false positives

■ Log events, including the following details:

   ■ Time/date

   ■ Sensor IP address

   ■ Manufacturer-specific attack name

   ■ Standard attack name (if one exists)

---

[70] Certain critical files, such as files storing user passwords and log files, will change regularly and thus should not be protected by a file integrity checker. This tendency will vary depending on the Web server and OS employed.

- ■ Source and destination IP addresses

- ■ Source and destination port numbers

- ■ Network protocol

- ■ For network events, capture packet header information to assist with the analysis and forensics process

- ■ Update with new attack signatures frequently (e.g., on a daily to weekly basis, typically after testing the updates).

In addition, it is critical that network-based IDPSs and their underlying OSs are hardened because network-based IDPSs are often a target of attackers. In particular, the network-based IDPSs should not respond to any type of system interrogation through their monitoring interfaces. If remote management is desired, it should be conducted through an out-of-band means (e.g., separate isolated network). Although sometimes difficult to administer and interpret, IDPSs are a critical early warning system that can provide the Web server administrator with the necessary information to defend the Web server from attack [NIST07].

8.2.3 Network Switches

Network switches are devices that provide connectivity between two or more hosts located on the same network segment. They are similar to hubs in that they allow communications between hosts, but, unlike hubs, the switches have more "intelligence" and send communications to only those hosts to which the communications are addressed. The benefit of this from a security standpoint is that when switches are employed on a network, it is much more difficult to eavesdrop on communications between other hosts on the network segment. This is extremely important when a Web server is on a network segment that is used by other hosts. For example, if a hub is used and a host on the DMZ is compromised, an attacker may be able to eavesdrop on the communications of other hosts on the DMZ, possibly leading to the compromise of those hosts or the information they communicate across the network. For example, e-mail servers in their default configurations receive unencrypted passwords; a compromise of the Web server would lead to the exposure of e-mail passwords by sniffing them from the compromised Web server.

Many switches include specific security settings that further enhance the security of the network by making it difficult for a malicious entity to "defeat" the switch. Some examples include the ability to minimize the risk of Address Resolution Protocol (ARP) spoofing and ARP poisoning attacks.[71] If a switch has these security capabilities, they should be enabled (see appropriate manufacturer documentation).

Switches can have a negative impact on network-based IDPSs (see Section 8.2.2). Most network switches allow network administrators to configure a specific port on the switch, known as a span port, so that it replicates all the switch's traffic to the port used by the IDPS. This allows a network-based IDPS to see all traffic on a particular network segment. However, under high loads, the switch might have to stop sending traffic to the span port, causing the IDPS to be unable to monitor network activity. Also, other devices use span ports, and there are typically very few span ports on a switch; therefore, it might not be possible to connect an IDPS to a particular switch because its span ports are all in use.

---

[71] ARP poisoning occurs when an attacker successfully updates the ARP cache on a target host with a forged ARP entry. This is generally used to redirect network traffic for malicious purposes.

8.2.4   Load Balancers

Load balancers distribute HTTP requests over multiple Web servers, allowing organizations to increase the capacity of their Web site by transparently adding additional servers. Load balancers act as virtual servers, receiving all HTTP requests to the Web site. These requests are forwarded, based on the load balancer's policy, to one of the servers that hosts the Web site. The load balancer's policy attempts to ensure that each server receives a similar number of requests. Many load balancers are capable of monitoring the servers and compensating if one of the servers becomes unavailable.

Load balancers are often augmented by caching mechanisms. Many of the HTTP requests an organization's Web server receives are identical and return identical HTTP responses. However, when dynamic content generation is in use, these identical responses need to be regenerated each time the request is made. To alleviate this requirement and further reduce the load on individual Web servers, organizations can deploy caching servers.

Like network switches, load balancers are not specifically security appliances, but they are essential tools for maintaining the availability of a Web site. By ensuring that several individual Web servers are sharing the load, rather than placing it on a single Web server, the organization is better able to withstand the high volume of requests used in many DoS attacks. Firewalls, switches, and routers should also be configured (when possible) to limit the amount of traffic that is passed to the Web servers, which further reduces the risk of successful DoS attacks.

8.2.5   Reverse Proxies

Reverse proxies are devices that sit between a Web server and the server's clients. The term "reverse proxy" is used because the data flow is the reverse of a traditional (forward) proxy. Reverse proxies can serve as a valuable addition to the security of a Web server. The term reverse proxy is used rather loosely in the industry and can include some or all of the following functionality:

■ Encryption accelerators, which off-load the computationally expensive processing required for initiating SSL/TLS connections

■ Security gateways, which monitor HTTP traffic to and from the Web server for potential attacks and take action as necessary, acting in essence as an application level firewall

■ Content filters, which can monitor traffic to and from the Web server for potentially sensitive or inappropriate data and take action as necessary

■ Authentication gateways, which authenticate users via a variety of mechanisms and control access to URLs hosted on the Web server itself.

Reverse proxies should be considered for any high-risk Web server deployment. While they do add risk by requiring the deployment of additional hardware and software, the risk is generally outweighed by the benefits. In addition to the functionality list above, Web proxies are also valuable because they add an additional layer between a Web server and its less trusted users. Due to their highly specialized nature, proxies are easier to secure than Web servers. Proxies also further obfuscate a Web server's configuration, type, location, and other details that are pertinent to attackers. For example, Web servers have banners that frequently reveal the Web server type and version, and these banners sometimes cannot be changed. With a reverse proxy, this is not an issue because the proxy can rewrite the banner before it is sent to users.

8.3   Checklist for Implementing a Secure Network Infrastructure

Completed	Action
	Identify network location
☐	Web server is located in a DMZ, or Web server hosting is outsourced
	Assess firewall configuration
☐	Web server is protected by a firewall; if it faces a higher threat or is more vulnerable, it is protected by an application layer firewall
☐	Firewall controls all traffic between the Internet and the Web server
☐	Firewall blocks all inbound traffic to the Web server except TCP ports 80 (HTTP) and/or 443 (HTTPS), if required
☐	Firewall blocks (in conjunction with the IDPS) IP addresses or subnets that the IDPS reports are attacking the organizational network
☐	Firewall notifies the network or Web server administrator of suspicious activity through an appropriate means
☐	Firewall provides content filtering (application layer firewall)
☐	Firewall is configured to protect against DoS attacks
☐	Firewall detects malformed or known attack URL requests
☐	Firewall logs critical events
☐	Firewall and firewall OS are patched to latest or most secure level
	Evaluate intrusion detection and prevention systems
☐	Host-based IDPS is used for Web servers that operate primarily using SSL/TLS
☐	IDPS is configured to monitor network traffic to and from the Web server after firewall
☐	IDPS is configured to monitor changes to critical files on Web server (host-based IDPS or file integrity checker)
☐	IDPS blocks (in conjunction with the firewall) IP addresses or subnets that are attacking the organizational network
☐	IDPS notifies the IDPS administrators or Web server administrator of attacks through appropriate means
☐	IDPS is configured to maximize detection with an acceptable level of false positives
☐	IDPS is configured to log events
☐	IDPS is updated with new attack signatures frequently (e.g., on a daily basis)
☐	Host-based IDPS is configured to monitor the system resources available in the Web server host
	Assess network switches
☐	Switches are used to protect against network eavesdropping
☐	Switches are configured in high-security mode to defeat ARP spoofing and ARP poisoning attacks
☐	Switches are configured to send all traffic on network segment to network-based IDPS
	Evaluate load balancers
☐	Load balancers are used to increase Web server availability
☐	Load balancers are augmented by Web caches if applicable
	Evaluate reverse proxies
☐	Reverse proxies are used as a security gateway to increase Web server availability
☐	Reverse proxies are augmented with encryption acceleration, user authentication, and content filtering capabilities, if applicable

9. Administering the Web Server

After initially deploying a Web server, administrators need to maintain its security continuously. This section provides general recommendations for securely administering Web servers. Vital activities include handling and analyzing log files, performing regular Web server backups, recovering from Web server compromises, testing Web server security regularly, and performing remote administration securely.

9.1 Logging

Logging is a cornerstone of a sound security posture. Capturing the correct data in the logs and then monitoring those logs closely is vital.[72] Network and system logs are important, especially system logs in the case of HTTPS-protected communications, where network monitoring is less effective. Web server software can provide additional log data relevant to Web-specific events. Similarly, Web applications may also maintain their own logs of actions.

Reviewing logs is mundane and reactive, and many Web server administrators devote their time to performing duties that they consider more important or urgent. However, log files are often the only record of suspicious behavior. Enabling the mechanisms to log information allows the logs to be used to detect failed and successful intrusion attempts and to initiate alert mechanisms when further investigation is needed. Procedures and tools need to be in place to process and analyze the log files and to review alert notifications.

Web server logs provide—

■ Alerts to suspicious activities that require further investigation

■ Tracking of an attacker's activities

■ Assistance in the recovery of the system

■ Assistance in post-event investigation

■ Required information for legal proceedings.

The selection and implementation of specific Web server software determines which set of detailed instructions (presented below) the Web server administrator should follow to establish logging configurations. Some of the information contained in the steps below may not be fully applicable to all manufacturers' Web server software products.

9.1.1 Identifying the Logging Capabilities of a Web Server

Each type of Web server software supports different logging capabilities. Depending on the Web server software used, one or more of the following logs may be available [Alle00]:

■ **Transfer Log**—Each transfer is represented as one entry showing the main information related to the transfer.

---

[72] For more information on logging, see NIST SP 800-92, *Guide to Computer Security Log Management*, which is available at http://csrc.nist.gov/publications/nistpubs/.

■ **Error Log**—Each error is represented as one entry, including an explanation of the reason for this error report.

■ **Agent Log**—This log contains information about the user client software used to access Web content.

■ **Referrer Log**—This log collects information relevant to HTTP access. This includes the URL of the page that contained the link that the user client software followed to initiate access to the Web page.

Most Web servers support the Transfer Log, and it is usually considered the most important. Several log formats are available for Transfer Log entries. Typically, the information is presented in plain American Standard Code for Information Interchange (ASCII) without special delimiters to separate the different fields [Alle00]:

■ **Common Log Format (CLF)**—This format stores information related to one transfer (Transfer Log) in the following order:

   ■ Remote host

   ■ Remote user identity in accordance with RFC 1413[73]

   ■ Authenticated user in accordance with the basic authentication scheme (see Section 7.3)

   ■ Date

   ■ URL requested

   ■ Status of the request

   ■ Number of bytes actually transferred.

■ **Combined Log Format**—This format contains the same seven fields above. It also provides information normally stored in the Agent Log and the Referrer Log, along with the actual transfer. Keeping this information in a consolidated log format may support more effective administration.

■ **Extended Log Format**—This format provides a way to describe all items that should be collected within the log file. The first two lines of the log file contain the version and the fields to be collected, and they appear in the log file as follows:

   #Version: 1.0
   #Fields: date time c-ip sc-bytes time-taken cs-version
   1999-08-01 02:10:57 192.0.0.2 6340 3 HTTP/1.0

   This example contains the date, time, originating address, number of bytes transmitted, time taken for transmission, and HTTP version.

■ **Other Log File Formats**—Some server software provides log information in different file formats, such as database formats or delimiter-separated formats. Other server software provides the

---

[73]   See the IETF Web site: http://www.ietf.org/rfc/rfc1413.txt.

capability for an administrator to define specific log file formats in the Web server configuration file using a particular syntax (if the default CLF format is insufficient).

9.1.2 Identifying Additional Logging Requirements

If a public Web server supports the execution of programs, scripts, or plug-ins, it may be necessary for the programs, scripts, or plug-ins to perform additional logging. Often, critical events take place within the Web application code itself and will not be logged by the Web server. If Webmasters develop or acquire application programs, scripts, or plug-ins, it is strongly recommended that they define and implement a comprehensive and easy-to-understand logging approach based on the logging mechanisms provided by the Web server host OS. Log information associated with programs, scripts, and plug-ins can add significantly to the typical information logged by the Web server and may prove invaluable when investigating events.

9.1.3 Recommended Generic Logging Configuration

The following configuration is a good starting point for logging into public Web servers [Alle00]:

- Use the combined log format for storing the Transfer Log, or manually configure the information described by the combined log format to be the standard format for the Transfer Log.

- Enable the Referrer Log or Agent Log if the combined log format is unavailable.

- Establish different log file names for different virtual Web sites that may be implemented as part of a single physical Web server.

- Use the remote user identity as specified in RFC 1413.

- Ensure procedures or mechanisms are in place so that log files do not fill up the hard drive.

Ensuring that sufficient log capacity is available is a concern because logs often take considerably more space than administrators initially estimate, especially when logging is set to a highly detailed level. Administrators should closely monitor the size of the log files when they implement different logging settings to ensure that the log files do not fill up the allocated storage. Because of the size of the log files, removing and archiving the logs more frequently or reducing the logging level of detail may be necessary.

Some Web server programs provide a capability to enforce or disable the checking of specified access controls during program startup. This level of control may be helpful, for example, to avoid inadvertent alteration of log files because of errors in file access administration. Web server administrators should determine the circumstances under which they may wish to enable such checks (assuming the Web server software supports this feature).

9.1.4 Reviewing and Retaining Log Files

Reviewing log files is a tedious and time-consuming task that informs administrators of events that have already occurred. Accordingly, files are often useful for corroborating other evidence, such as a CPU utilization spike or anomalous network traffic reported by an IDPS. When a log is used to corroborate other evidence, a focused review is in order. For example, if an IDPS reported an outbound FTP connection from the Web server at 8:17 a.m., then a review of the logs generated around 8:17 a.m. is appropriate. Web server logs should also be reviewed for indications of attacks. The frequency of the reviews depends on the following factors:

■ Amount of traffic the server receives

■ General threat level (certain sites receive many more attacks than other sites and thus should have their logs reviewed more frequently)

■ Specific threats (at certain times, specific threats arise that may require more frequent log file analysis)

■ Vulnerability of the Web server

■ Value of data and services provided by the Web server.

Reviews should take place regularly (e.g., daily) and when a suspicious activity has been noted or a threat warning has been issued. Obviously, the task could quickly become burdensome to a Web server administrator. To reduce this burden, automated log analysis tools have been developed (see Section 9.1.5).

In addition, a long-term and more in-depth analysis of the logs is needed. Because a typical Web server attack can involve hundreds of unique requests, an attacker may attempt to disguise a Web server attack by increasing the interval between requests. In this case, reviewing a single day's or week's logs may not show recognizable trends. However, when trends are analyzed over a week, month, or quarter, multiple attacks from the same host or subnet can be more easily recognized.

Log files should be protected to ensure that if an attacker does compromise a Web server, the log files cannot be altered to cover the attack. Although encryption can be useful in protecting log files, the best solution is to store log files on a host separate from the Web server. This is often called a centralized logging server. Centralized logging is often performed using syslog, which is a standard logging protocol.[74] Alternately, some organizations use security information and event management (SIEM) software that uses centralized servers to perform log analysis, database servers to store logs, and either agents installed on the individual hosts or processes running on the centralized servers to transfer Web server logs or log data from the hosts to the servers and parse the logs.[75]

Log files should be backed up and archived regularly. Archiving log files for a period of time is important for several reasons, including supporting certain legal actions and troubleshooting problems with the Web server. The retention period for archived log files depends on a number of factors, including the following:

■ Legal requirements

■ Organizational requirements

■ Size of logs (which is directly related to the traffic of the site and the number of details logged)

■ Value of Web server data and services

■ Threat level.

---

[74] Syslog is defined in IETF RFC 3164, *The BSD Syslog Protocol*, which is available at http://www.ietf.org/rfc/rfc3164.txt.
[75] More information on syslog and SIEM implementations is provided in NIST SP 800-92, *Guide to Computer Security Log Management*, which is available at http://csrc.nist.gov/publications/nistpubs/.

9.1.5 Automated Log File Analysis Tools

Most public Web servers receive significant amounts of traffic, and the log files quickly become voluminous. Automated log analysis tools should be installed to ease the burden on the Web server administrator. These tools analyze the entries in the Web server log files and identify suspicious and unusual activity. As mentioned in Section 9.1.2, some organizations use SIEM software for centralized logging, which can also perform automated log file analysis.

Many commercial and public domain tools are available to support regular analysis of Transfer Logs. Most operate on either the common or the combined log formats. These tools can identify IP addresses that are the source of high numbers of connections and transfers.

Error Log tools indicate not only errors that may exist within available Web content (such as missing files) but also attempts to access nonexistent URLs. Such attempts could indicate the following:

■ Probes for the existence of vulnerabilities to be used later in launching an attack

■ Information gathering

■ Interest in specific content, such as databases.

The automated log analyzer should forward any suspicious events to the responsible Web server administrator or security incident response team as soon as possible for follow-up investigation. Some organizations may wish to use two or more log analyzers, which will reduce the risk of missing an attacker or other significant events in the log files [NIST06b].

9.2 Web Server Backup Procedures

One of the most important functions of a Web server administrator is to maintain the integrity of the data on the Web server. This is important because Web servers are often some of the most exposed and vital servers on an organization's network. There are two principal components to backing up data on a Web server: regular backup of the data and OS on the Web server, and maintenance of a separate protected authoritative copy of the organization's Web content.

9.2.1 Web Server Backup Policies and Strategies

The Web server administrator needs to perform backups of the Web server on a regular basis for several reasons. A Web server could fail as a result of a malicious or unintentional act or a hardware or software failure. In addition, Federal agencies and many other organizations are governed by regulations on the backup and archiving of Web server data. Web server data should also be backed up regularly for legal and financial reasons.

All organizations need to create a Web server data backup policy. Three main factors influence the contents of this policy:

■ Legal requirements

  ■ Applicable laws and regulations (Federal, state, and international)

  ■ Litigation requirements

■ Mission requirements

- ■ Contractual

- ■ Accepted practices

- ■ Criticality of data to organization

- ■ Organizational guidelines and policies.

Although each organization's Web server backup policy will be different to reflect its particular environment, it should address the following issues:

- ■ Purpose of the policy

- ■ Parties affected by the policy

- ■ Web servers covered by the policy

- ■ Definitions of key terms, especially legal and technical

- ■ Detailed requirements from the legal, business, and organization's perspective

- ■ Required frequency of backups

- ■ Procedures for ensuring data is properly retained and protected

- ■ Procedures for ensuring data is properly destroyed or archived when no longer required

- ■ Procedures for preserving information for Freedom of Information Act (FOIA) requests, legal investigations, and other such requests

- ■ Responsibilities of those involved in data retention, protection, and destruction activities

- ■ Retention period for each type of information logged[76]

- ■ Specific duties of a central/organizational data backup team, if one exists.

Three primary types of backups exist: full, incremental, and differential. Full backups include the OS, applications, and data stored on the Web server (i.e., an image of every piece of data stored on the Web server hard drives). The advantage of a full backup is that it is easy to restore the entire Web server to the state (e.g., configuration, patch level, data) it was in when the backup was performed. The disadvantage of full backups is that they take considerable time and resources to perform. Incremental backups reduce the impact of backups by backing up only data that has changed since the previous backup (either full or incremental).

Differential backups reduce the number of backup sets that must be accessed to restore a configuration by backing up all changed data since the last full backup. However, each differential backup increases as

---

[76] Organizations should carefully consider the retention period for Web transaction logs and other Web server-related records. Many organizations are subject to multiple sets of legal and regulatory requirements that can affect their retention of Web records. The National Archives and Records Administration (NARA) has a Web site for Federal records management, which is located at http://www.archives.gov/records-mgmt/.

time lapses from the last full backup, requiring more processing time and storage than would an incremental backup. Generally, full backups are performed less frequently (weekly to monthly or when a significant change occurs), and incremental or differential backups are performed more frequently (daily to weekly). The frequency of backups will be determined by several factors:

- Volatility of information on the Web site

    - Static Web content (less frequent backups)

    - Dynamic Web content (more frequent backups)

    - E-commerce/e-government (very frequent backups)

- Volatility of configuring the Web server

- Amount of data to be backed up

- Backup device and media available

- Time available for dumping backup data

- Criticality of data

- Threat level faced by the Web server

- Effort required for data reconstruction without data backup

- Other data backup or redundancy features of the Web server (e.g., Redundant Array of Inexpensive Disks [RAID]).

9.2.2 Maintain a Test Web Server

Most organizations will probably wish to maintain a test or development Web server. Ideally, this server should have hardware and software identical to the production or live Web server and be located on an internal network segment (intranet) where it can be fully protected by the organization's perimeter network defenses. Although the cost of maintaining an additional Web server is not inconsequential, having a test Web server offers numerous advantages:

- It provides a platform to test new patches and service packs prior to application on the production Web server.

- It provides a development platform for the Webmaster and Web server administrator to develop and test new content and applications.

- It provides a platform to test configuration settings before applying them to production Web servers.

- Software critical for development and testing but that might represent an unacceptable security risk on the production server can be installed on the development server (e.g., software compliers, administrative tool kits, remote access software).

The test Web server should be separate from the server that maintains an authoritative copy of the content on the production Web server (see Section 9.2.3).

9.2.3 Maintain an Authoritative Copy of Organizational Web Content

All organizations should maintain an authoritative (i.e., verified and trusted) copy of their public Web sites on a host that is inaccessible to the Internet. This is a supplement to, but not replacement for, an appropriate backup policy (see Section 9.2.1). For simple, relatively static Web sites, this could be as simple as a copy of the Web site on a read-only medium (e.g., Compact Disc-Recordable [CD-R]). However, for most organizations, the authoritative copy of the Web site is maintained on a secure host. This host is usually located behind the organization's firewall on the internal network and not on the DMZ (see Section 8.1.2). The purpose of the authoritative copy is to provide a means of restoring information on the public Web server if it is compromised as a result of an accident or malicious action. This authoritative copy of the Web site allows an organization to rapidly recover from Web site integrity breaches (e.g., defacement).

To successfully accomplish the goal of providing and protecting an authoritative copy of the Web server content, the following requirements must be met:

■ Protect authoritative copy from unauthorized access.

  ■ Use write-once media (appropriate for relatively static Web sites).

  ■ Locate the host with the authoritative copy behind a firewall, and ensure there is no outside access to the host.

  ■ Minimize users with authorized access to host.

  ■ Control user access in as granular a manner as possible.

  ■ Employ strong user authentication.

  ■ Employ appropriate logging and monitoring procedures.

  ■ Consider additional authoritative copies at different physical locations for further protection.

■ Establish appropriate authoritative copy update procedures.

  ■ Update authoritative copy first (any testing on code should occur before updating the authoritative copy).

  ■ Establish policies and procedures for who can authorize updates, who can perform updates, when updates can occur, etc.

■ Establish a process for copying authoritative copy to a production Web server.

  ■ Physically transfer data using secure physical media (e.g., encrypted and/or write-once media, such as CD-Rs).

  ■ Use a secure protocol (e.g., SSH) for network transfers.

■ Include the procedures for restoring from the authoritative copy in the organizational incident response procedures (see Section 9.3).

■ Consider performing automatic updates from the authoritative copy to the Web server periodically (e.g., every 15 minutes, hourly, or daily) because this will overwrite a Web site defacement automatically.

9.3 Recovering From a Security Compromise

Most organizations eventually face a successful compromise of one or more hosts on their network. The first step in recovering from a compromise is to create and document the required policies and procedures for responding to successful intrusions *before* an intrusion.[77] The response procedures should outline the actions that are required to respond to a successful compromise of the Web server and the appropriate sequence of these actions (sequence can be critical). Most organizations already have a dedicated incident response team in place, which should be contacted immediately when there is suspicion or confirmation of a compromise. In addition, the organization may wish to ensure that some of its staff are knowledgeable in the fields of computer and network forensics.[78]

A Web server administrator should follow the organization's policies and procedures for incident handling, and the incident response team should be contacted for guidance before the organization takes any action after a suspected or confirmed security compromise. Examples of steps commonly performed after discovering a successful compromise are as follows:

■ Report the incident to the organization's computer incident response capability.

■ Isolate the compromised systems or take other steps to contain the attack so that additional information can be collected.[79]

■ Consult expeditiously, as appropriate, with management, legal counsel, and law enforcement.

■ Investigate similar[80] hosts to determine if the attacker also has compromised other systems.

■ Analyze the intrusion, including—

■ The current state of the server, starting with the most ephemeral data (e.g., current network connections, memory dump, files time stamps, logged in users)

■ Modifications made to the system's software and configuration

■ Modifications made to the data

■ Tools or data left behind by the attacker

■ System, intrusion detection, and firewall log files.

---

[77] For more information on this area, see NIST SP 800-61, *Computer Security Incident Handling Guide,* and NIST SP 800-18 Revision 1, *Guide for Developing Security Plans for Federal Information Systems* (http://csrc.nist.gov/publications/nistpubs/).

[78] More information on computer and network forensics is available from NIST SP 800-86, *Guide to Integrating Forensic Techniques Into Incident Response* (http://csrc.nist.gov/publications/nistpubs/).

[79] Isolating the system must be accomplished with great care if the organization wishes to collect evidence. Many attackers configure compromised systems to erase evidence if a compromised system is disconnected from the network or rebooted. One method to isolate a system would be to reconfigure the nearest upstream switch or router.

[80] Similar hosts would include hosts that are in the same IP address range, have the same or similar passwords, share a trust relationship, and/or have the same OS and/or applications.

- Restore the system.

  - Either install a clean version of the OS, applications, necessary patches, and Web content; or restore the system from backups (this option can be more risky because the backups may have been made after the compromise, and restoring from a compromised backup may still allow the attacker access to the system).

  - Disable unnecessary services.

  - Apply all patches.

  - Change all passwords (including on uncompromised hosts, if their passwords are believed to have been seen by the compromised host, or if the same passwords are used on other hosts).

  - Reconfigure network security elements (e.g., firewall, router, IDPS) to provide additional protection and notification.

- Test system to ensure security.

- Reconnect system to network.

- Monitor system and network for signs that the attacker is attempting to access the system or network again.

- Document lessons learned.

Based on the organization's policy and procedures, system administrators should decide whether to reinstall the OS of a compromised system or restore it from a backup. Factors that are often considered include the following:

- Level of access that the attacker gained (e.g., root, user, guest, system)

- Type of attacker (internal or external)

- Purpose of compromise (e.g., Web page defacement, illegal software repository, platform for other attacks)

- Method used for the system compromise

- Actions of the attacker during and after the compromise (e.g., log files, intrusion detection reports)

- Duration of the compromise

- Extent of the compromise on the network (e.g., the number of hosts compromised)

- Results of consultation with management and legal counsel.

The lower the level of access gained by the intruder and the more the Web server administrator understands about the attacker's actions, the less risk there is in restoring from a backup and patching the vulnerability. For incidents in which there is less known about the attacker's actions and/or in which the attacker gains high-level access, it is recommended that the OS and applications be reinstalled from the manufacturer's original distribution media and that the Web server data be restored from a known good backup.

If legal action is pursued, system administrators need to be aware of the guidelines for handling a host after a compromise. Consult legal counsel and relevant law enforcement authorities as appropriate.

9.4 Security Testing Web Servers

Periodic security testing of public Web servers is critical. Without periodic testing, there is no assurance that current protective measures are working or that the security patch applied by the Web server administrator is functioning as advertised. Although a variety of security testing techniques exists, vulnerability scanning is the most common. Vulnerability scanning assists a Web server administrator in identifying vulnerabilities and verifying whether the existing security measures are effective. Penetration testing is also used, but it is used less frequently and usually only as part of an overall penetration test of the organization's network.[81]

9.4.1 Vulnerability Scanning

Vulnerability scanners are automated tools that are used to identify vulnerabilities and misconfigurations of hosts. Many vulnerability scanners also provide information about mitigating discovered vulnerabilities.

Vulnerability scanners attempt to identify vulnerabilities in the hosts scanned. Vulnerability scanners can help identify out-of-date software versions, missing patches, or system upgrades, and they can validate compliance with or deviations from the organization's security policy. To accomplish this, vulnerability scanners identify OSs and major software applications running on hosts and match them with known vulnerabilities in their vulnerability databases.

However, vulnerability scanners have some significant weaknesses. Generally, they identify only surface vulnerabilities and are unable to address the overall risk level of a scanned Web server. Although the scan process itself is highly automated, vulnerability scanners can have a high false positive error rate (reporting vulnerabilities when none exist). This means an individual with expertise in Web server security and administration must interpret the results. Furthermore, vulnerability scanners cannot generally identify vulnerabilities in custom code or applications.

Vulnerability scanners rely on periodic updating of the vulnerability database to recognize the latest vulnerabilities. Before running any scanner, Web server administrators should install the latest updates to its vulnerability database. Some databases are updated more regularly than others (the frequency of updates should be a major consideration when choosing a vulnerability scanner).

Vulnerability scanners are often better at detecting well-known vulnerabilities than more esoteric ones because it is impossible for any one scanning product to incorporate all known vulnerabilities in a timely manner. In addition, manufacturers want to keep the speed of their scanners high (the more vulnerabilities detected, the more tests required, which slows the overall scanning process). Therefore, vulnerability scanners may be less useful to Web server administrators operating less popular Web servers, OSs, or custom-coded applications.

Vulnerability scanners provide the following capabilities:

---

[81] For information about other testing techniques, see NIST SP 800-42, *Guideline on Network Security Testing* (http://csrc.nist.gov/publications/nistpubs/).

■ Identifying active hosts on a network

■ Identifying active services (ports) on hosts and which of these are vulnerable

■ Identifying applications and banner grabbing

■ Identifying OSs

■ Identifying vulnerabilities associated with discovered OSs and applications

■ Testing compliance with host application usage/security policies.

Organizations should conduct vulnerability scanning to validate that OSs and Web server applications are up-to-date on security patches and software versions. Vulnerability scanning is a labor-intensive activity that requires a high degree of human involvement to interpret the results. It may also be disruptive to operations by taking up network bandwidth, slowing network response times, and potentially affecting the availability of the scanned server or its applications. However, vulnerability scanning is extremely important for ensuring that vulnerabilities are mitigated as soon as possible, before they are discovered and exploited by adversaries. Vulnerability scanning should be conducted on a weekly to monthly basis. Many organizations also run a vulnerability scan whenever a new vulnerability database is released for the organization's scanner application. Vulnerability scanning results should be documented and discovered deficiencies should be corrected.

Organizations should also consider running more than one vulnerability scanner. As previously discussed, no scanner is able to detect all known vulnerabilities; however, using two scanners generally increases the number of vulnerabilities detected. A common practice is to use one commercial and one freeware scanner. Network-based and host-based vulnerability scanners are available for free or for a fee.

9.4.2 Penetration Testing

"Penetration testing is security testing in which evaluators attempt to circumvent the security features of a system based on their understanding of the system design and implementation" [NISS99]. The purpose of penetration testing is to exercise system protections (particularly human response to attack indications) by using common tools and techniques developed by attackers. This testing is highly recommended for complex or critical systems.

Penetration testing can be an invaluable technique to any organization's information security program. However, it is a very labor-intensive activity and requires great expertise to minimize the risk to targeted systems. At a minimum, it may slow the organization's network response time because of network mapping and vulnerability scanning. Furthermore, the possibility exists that systems may be damaged or rendered inoperable in the course of penetration testing. Although this risk is mitigated by the use of experienced penetration testers, it can never be fully eliminated.

Penetration testing does offer the following benefits [NIST02b]:

■ Tests the network using the same methodologies and tools employed by attackers

■ Verifies whether vulnerabilities exist

■ Goes beyond surface vulnerabilities and demonstrates how these vulnerabilities can be exploited iteratively to gain greater access

■ Demonstrates that vulnerabilities are not purely theoretical

■ Provides the "realism" necessary to address security issues

■ Allows for testing of procedures and susceptibility of the human element to social engineering.

9.5 Remotely Administering a Web Server

It is strongly recommended that remote administration and remote updating of content for a Web server be allowed only after careful consideration of the risks. The most secure configuration is to disallow any remote administration or content updates. However, that might not be viable for all organizations. The risk of enabling remote administration or content updates varies considerably depending on the location of the Web server on the network (see Section 8.1). For a Web server that is located behind a firewall, remote administration or content updating can be implemented relatively securely from the internal network, but not without added risk. Remote administration or content updating should generally not be allowed from a host located outside the organization's network unless it is performed from an organization-controlled computer through the organization's remote access solution, such as a VPN.

If an organization determines that it is necessary to remotely administer or update content on a Web server, following these steps should ensure that content is implemented in as secure a manner as possible:

■ Use a strong authentication mechanism (e.g., public/private key pair, two-factor authentication).

■ Restrict which hosts can be used to remotely administer or update content on the Web server.

   ■ Restrict by authorized users

   ■ Restrict by IP address (not hostname)

   ■ Restrict to hosts on the internal network or those using the organization's enterprise remote access solution.

■ Use secure protocols that can provide encryption of both passwords and data (e.g., SSH, HTTPS); do not use less secure protocols (e.g., telnet, FTP, NFS, HTTP) unless absolutely required and tunneled over an encrypted protocol, such as SSH, SSL, or IPsec.

■ Enforce the concept of least privilege on remote administration and content updating (e.g., attempt to minimize the access rights for the remote administration/update accounts).

■ Do not allow remote administration from the Internet through the firewall unless accomplished via strong mechanisms, such as VPNs.

■ Change any default accounts or passwords for the remote administration utility or application.

■ Do not mount any file shares on the internal network from the Web server or vice versa.

9.6 Checklist for Administering the Web Server

Completed	Action
	Perform logging
☐	Use the combined log format for storing the Transfer Log or manually configure the information described by the combined log format to be the standard format for the Transfer Log
☐	Enable the Referrer Log or Agent Log if the combined log format is unavailable
☐	Establish different log file names for different virtual Web sites that may be implemented as part of a single physical Web server
☐	Use the remote user identity as specified in RFC 1413
☐	Store logs on a separate (syslog) host
☐	Ensure there is sufficient capacity for the logs
☐	Archive logs according to organizational requirements
☐	Review logs daily
☐	Review logs weekly (for more long-term trends)
☐	Use automated log file analysis tool(s)
	Perform Web server backups
☐	Create a Web server backup policy
☐	Back up Web server differentially or incrementally on a daily to weekly basis
☐	Back up Web server fully on a weekly to monthly basis
☐	Periodically archive backups
☐	Maintain an authoritative copy of Web site(s)
	Recover from a compromise
☐	Report the incident to the organization's computer incident response capability
☐	Isolate the compromised system(s) or take other steps to contain the attack so additional information can be collected
☐	Investigate similar hosts to determine if the attacker has also compromised other systems
☐	Consult, as appropriate, with management, legal counsel, and law enforcement officials expeditiously
☐	Analyze the intrusion
☐	Restore the system
☐	Test system to ensure security
☐	Reconnect system to network
☐	Monitor system and network for signs that the attacker is attempting to access the system or network again
☐	Document lessons learned
	Test security
☐	Periodically conduct vulnerability scans on Web server, dynamically generated content, and supporting network
☐	Update vulnerability scanner prior to testing
☐	Correct any deficiencies identified by the vulnerability scanner
☐	Conduct penetration testing on the Web server and the supporting network infrastructure
☐	Correct deficiencies identified by penetration testing

Completed	Action
	Conduct remote administration and content updates
☐	Use a strong authentication mechanism (e.g., public/private key pair, two-factor authentication)
☐	Restrict hosts that can be used to remotely administer or update content on the Web server by IP address and to the internal network
☐	Use secure protocols (e.g., SSH, HTTPS)
☐	Enforce the concept of least privilege on remote administration and content updating (e.g., attempt to minimize the access rights for the remote administration/update accounts)
☐	Change any default accounts or passwords from the remote administration utility or application
☐	Do not allow remote administration from the Internet unless mechanisms such as VPNs are used
☐	Do not mount any file shares on the internal network from the Web server or vice versa

Appendix A—Online Web Server Security Resources

This appendix contains lists of online resources that may be helpful to Web server administrators and others in achieving a greater understanding of Web server security and in securing their Web servers.

Active Content Security Resources

Resource/Title	URL
Active Software Professionals (ASP) Alliance	http://www.aspalliance.com/
cgisecurity.net	http://www.cgisecurity.com/lib/
Department of Homeland Security (DHS) Build Security In Portal	https://buildsecurityin.us-cert.gov/
Exploiting Common Vulnerabilities in PHP Hypertext Preprocessor (PHP) Applications	http://www.securereality.com.au/studyinscarlet.txt
Java SE Security	http://java.sun.com/security/
The Official Microsoft ASP.NET 2.0 Site	http://www.asp.net/
Open Web Application Security Project (OWASP)	http://www.owasp.org/
OWASP Top Ten	http://www.owasp.org/index.php/Category:OWASP_Top_Ten_Project
PHP Security Guide	http://phpsec.org/php-security-guide.pdf
Web Application Security Consortium	http://www.webappsec.org/

Apache Web Server Security Resources

Resource/Title	URL
Apache 1.3 Security Tips	http://httpd.apache.org/docs/1.3/misc/security_tips.html
Apache 2.0 Security Tips	http://httpd.apache.org/docs/2.0/misc/security_tips.html
Apache 2.2 Security Tips	http://httpd.apache.org/docs/2.2/misc/security_tips.html
Apache Secure Sockets Layer (SSL)	http://www.apache-ssl.org/
Apache Tutorials	http://httpd.apache.org/docs/misc/tutorials.html
Apache-server.com	http://apache-server.com/
Securing Apache	http://www.adobe.com/v1/documentcenter/partners/asz_aswps_securing_apache.pdf
Securing Apache: Step-by-Step	http://www.securityfocus.com/infocus/1694
Securing Apache 2: Step-by-Step	http://www.securityfocus.com/infocus/1786
Securing Your Web Pages With Apache	http://apache-server.com/tutorials/LPauth1.html

Application Assessment and Code Review Resources

Resource/Title	URL
Detecting Web Application Security Vulnerabilities	http://www.oreillynet.com/pub/a/sysadmin/2006/11/02/webapp_security_scans.html
DHS Build Security In Portal	https://buildsecurityin.us-cert.gov/
OWASP WebGoat	http://www.owasp.org/index.php/OWASP_WebGoat_Project
OWASP WebScarab	http://www.owasp.org/index.php/OWASP_WebScarab_Project
A Process for Performing Security Code Reviews	http://www.computer.org/portal/site/security/index.jsp?pageID=security_level1_article&TheCat=1001&path=security/2006/v4n4&file=basic.xml
SPI Dynamics	http://www.spidynamics.com/
Wapiti	http://wapiti.sourceforge.net/
Watchfire	http://www.watchfire.com/
Web Application Security Consortium Articles	http://www.webappsec.org/projects/articles/

Digital Certificate Providers (Third-Party Certificate Authorities)

Resource/Title	URL
CertiSign Certificadora Digital Ltda	http://www.certisign.com.br/
Deutsches Forschungsnetz	http://www.pca.dfn.de/
Entrust.net Ltd.	http://www.entrust.net/
GeoTrust Inc.	http://www.geotrust.com/
GlobalSign NV/SA	http://www.globalsign.net/
GoDaddy	http://www.godaddy.com/
IKS GmbH	http://www.iks-jena.de/produkte/ca/
IdenTrust	http://www.identrust.com/
Lanechange.net	http://www.lanechange.net/
Register.com	http://www.register.com/
TC TrustCenter	http://www.trustcenter.de/
Thawte	http://www.thawte.com/certs/server/request.html
VeriSign	http://www.verisign.com/

General Web Server Security Resources

Resource/Title	URL
A Look Into Web Server and Web Application Attack Signatures	http://www.cgisecurity.com/papers/fingerprint-port80.txt
Center for Education and Research in Information Assurance and Security (CERIAS)	http://www.cerias.purdue.edu/
Computer Emergency Response Team Coordination Center (CERT/CC), Securing Public Web Servers	http://www.sei.cmu.edu/pub/documents/sims/pdf/sim011.pdf

Resource/Title	URL
CERT	http://www.cert.org/
Department of Defense (DoD) Web Site Administration Policies and Procedures	http://www.defenselink.mil/webmasters/policy/dod_web_policy_12071998_with_amendments_and_corrections.html
National Information Assurance Partnership	http://www.nsa.gov/ia/industry/niap.cfm
National Institute of Standards and Technology (NIST) Computer Security Resource Center	http://csrc.nist.gov/
NIST National Vulnerability Database	http://nvd.nist.gov/
Office of Management and Budget Circular No. A-130	http://www.whitehouse.gov/omb/circulars/a130/a130.html
Open Source Vulnerability Database	http://www.osvdb.org/
RISKS Forum	http://catless.ncl.ac.uk/Risks/
SANS Institute	http://www.sans.org/
SANS Top-20 Internet Security Attack Targets	http://www.sans.org/top20.htm
Security Configuration Checklists Program for IT Products	http://checklists.nist.gov/
Trust Management on the World Wide Web	http://www.firstmonday.dk/issues/issue3_6/khare/
U.S. Department of Energy Computer Incident Advisory Capability (CIAC)	http://www.ciac.org/ciac/
United States Computer Emergency Response Team (US-CERT)	http://www.us-cert.gov/
World Wide Web Security Frequently Asked Questions	http://www.w3.org/Security/Faq/www-security-faq.html

Internet Information Services (IIS) Web Server Security Resources

Resource/Title	URL
eEye Advisories and Alerts	http://research.eeye.com/html/advisories/published/index.html
IIS 5.0 Security Checklist	http://www.microsoft.com/technet/prodtechnol/windows2000serv/technologies/iis/tips/iis5chk.mspx
IIS 6 Security	http://www.securityfocus.com/infocus/1765
IIS 6 Security Best Practices	http://technet2.microsoft.com/WindowsServer/en/library/ace052a0-a713-423e-8e8c-4bf198f597b81033.mspx
IIS Lockdown Tool	http://www.microsoft.com/technet/security/tools/locktool.mspx
National Security Agency (NSA) Guide to the Secure Configuration and Administration of Microsoft IIS 5.0	http://www.nsa.gov/notices/notic00004.cfm?Address=/snac/os/win2k/iis_5_v1_4.pdf
Security in IIS 6.0	http://www.microsoft.com/technet/prodtechnol/WindowsServer2003/Library/IIS/f8f81568-31f2-4210-9982-b9391afc30eb.mspx?mfr=true

Miscellaneous Web Security Resources

Resource/Title	URL
dominosecurity.org	http://www.dominosecurity.org/
Honeynet Project	http://project.honeynet.org/
Lotus Domino Security Page	http://www-128.ibm.com/developerworks/lotus/security/
Microsoft Internet Explorer Home Page	http://www.microsoft.com/windows/products/winfamily/ie/default.mspx
Mozilla Security Center	http://www.mozilla.org/security/
Netcraft	http://www.netcraft.com/

Phishing Resources

Resource/Title	URL
Anti-Phishing Working Group (APWG)	http://www.antiphishing.org/
Federal Trade Commission (FTC), "How Not to Get Hooked by a 'Phishing' Scam"	http://www.ftc.gov/bcp/edu/pubs/consumer/alerts/alt127.htm
Internet Crime Complaint Center (ICCC)	http://www.ic3.gov/
Phish Report Network	http://www.phishreport.net/

WebBot Information

Resource/Title	URL
BotSpot	http://www.botspot.com
Configuring the robots.txt Files	http://www.robotstxt.org/wc/exclusion.html#robotstxt
NIST Mobile Agent Security	http://csrc.nist.gov/mobileagents/projects.html
Showing Robots the Door	http://www.ariadne.ac.uk/issue15/robots/
University of Maryland Baltimore County (UMBC) AgentWeb	http://agents.umbc.edu/

NIST Publications on System and Network Security[82]

Publication	URL
SP 800-18 Revision 1, *Guide for Developing Security Plans for Federal Information Systems*	http://csrc.nist.gov/publications/nistpubs/800-18-Rev1/sp800-18-Rev1-final.pdf
SP 800-26, *Security Self-Assessment Guide for Information Technology Systems*	http://csrc.nist.gov/publications/nistpubs/800-26/sp800-26.pdf
SP 800-27, *Engineering Principles for Information Technology Security*	http://csrc.nist.gov/publications/nistpubs/800-27A/SP800-27-RevA.pdf
SP 800-28 Version 2 (DRAFT), *Guidelines on Active Content and Mobile Code*	http://csrc.nist.gov/publications/nistpubs/

[82] The primary Web site for all of these publications is located at http://csrc.nist.gov/publications/index.html.

Publication	URL
SP 800-32, *Introduction to Public Key Technology and the Federal PKI Infrastructure*	http://csrc.nist.gov/publications/nistpubs/800-32/sp800-32.pdf
SP 800-34, *Contingency Planning Guide for Information Technology Systems*	http://csrc.nist.gov/publications/nistpubs/800-34/sp800-34.pdf
SP 800-37, *Guide for the Security Certification and Accreditation of Federal Information Systems*	http://csrc.nist.gov/publications/nistpubs/800-37/SP800-37-final.pdf
SP 800-40 Version 2, *Creating a Patch and Vulnerability Management Program*	http://csrc.nist.gov/publications/nistpubs/800-40-Ver2/SP800-40v2.pdf
SP 800-41, *Guidelines on Firewalls and Firewall Policy*	http://csrc.nist.gov/publications/nistpubs/800-41/sp800-41.pdf
SP 800-42, *Guideline on Network Security Testing*	http://csrc.nist.gov/publications/nistpubs/800-42/NIST-SP800-42.pdf
SP 800-45 Version 2, *Guidelines on Electronic Mail Security*	http://csrc.nist.gov/publications/nistpubs/800-45-version2/SP800-45v2.pdf
SP 800-46, *Security for Telecommuting and Broadband Communications*	http://csrc.nist.gov/publications/nistpubs/800-46/sp800-46.pdf
SP 800-52, *Guidelines for the Selection and Use of Transport Layer Security (TLS) Implementations*	http://csrc.nist.gov/publications/nistpubs/800-52/SP800-52.pdf
SP 800-53 Revision 1, *Recommended Security Controls for Federal Information Systems*	http://csrc.nist.gov/publications/nistpubs/800-53-Rev1/800-53-rev1-final-clean-sz.pdf
SP 800-61, *Computer Security Incident Handling Guide*	http://csrc.nist.gov/publications/nistpubs/800-61/sp800-61.pdf
SP 800-63, *Electronic Authentication Guideline*	http://csrc.nist.gov/publications/nistpubs/800-63/SP800-63V1_0_2.pdf
SP 800-68, *Guidance for Securing Microsoft Windows XP Systems for IT Professionals*	http://csrc.nist.gov/itsec/download_WinXP.html
SP 800-69, *Guidance for Securing Microsoft Windows XP Home Edition: A NIST Security Configuration Checklist*	http://csrc.nist.gov/itsec/guidance_WinXP_Home.html
SP 800-77, *Guide to IPsec VPNs*	http://csrc.nist.gov/publications/nistpubs/800-77/sp800-77.pdf
SP 800-81, *Secure Domain Name System (DNS) Deployment Guide*	http://csrc.nist.gov/publications/nistpubs/800-81/SP800-81.pdf
SP 800-83, *Guide to Malware Incident Prevention and Handling*	http://csrc.nist.gov/publications/nistpubs/800-83/SP800-83.pdf
SP 800-86, *Guide to Integrating Forensic Techniques into Incident Response*	http://csrc.nist.gov/publications/nistpubs/800-86/SP800-86.pdf
SP 800-92, *Guide to Computer Security Log Management*	http://csrc.nist.gov/publications/nistpubs/800-92/SP800-92.pdf
SP 800-94, *Guide to Intrusion Detection and Prevention Systems (IDPS)*	http://csrc.nist.gov/publications/nistpubs/800-94/SP800-94.pdf
SP 800-95, *Guide to Secure Web Services*	http://csrc.nist.gov/publications/nistpubs/800-95/SP800-95.pdf

Appendix B—Glossary

Address Resolution Protocol (ARP)—A protocol used to obtain a node's physical address. A client station broadcasts an ARP request onto the network with the Internet Protocol (IP) address of the target node with which it wishes to communicate, and with that address the node responds by sending back its physical address so that packets can be transmitted to it.

Content Generator—A program on a Web server that will dynamically generate HyperText Markup Language (HTML) pages for users. Content generators can range from simple Common Gateway Interface (CGI) scripts executed by the Web server to Java EE or .NET application servers in which most—if not all—HTML pages served are dynamically generated.

Demilitarized Zone (DMZ)—A host or network segment inserted as a "neutral zone" between an organization's private network and the Internet.

Host—Almost any kind of computer, including a centralized mainframe that is a host to its terminals, a server that is host to its clients, or a desktop personal computer (PC) that is host to its peripherals. In network architectures, a client station (user's machine) is also considered a host because it is a source of information to the network, in contrast to a device, such as a router or switch, that directs traffic.

Hotfix—Microsoft's term for "patch."

Mandatory Access Control—A means of restricting access to system resources based on the sensitivity (as represented by a label) of the information contained in the system resource and the formal authorization (i.e., clearance) of users to access information of such sensitivity.

Network Administrator—A person who manages a local area network (LAN) within an organization. Responsibilities include ensuring network security, installing new applications, distributing software upgrades, monitoring daily activity, enforcing licensing agreements, developing a storage management program, and providing for routine backups.

Nonce—A randomly generated value used to defeat "playback" attacks in communication protocols. One party randomly generates a nonce and sends it to the other party. The receiver encrypts it using the agreed upon secret key and returns it to the sender. Because the sender randomly generated the nonce, this defeats playback attacks because the replayer cannot know in advance the nonce the sender will generate. The receiver denies connections that do not have the correctly encrypted nonce.

Operating System—The software "master control application" that runs the computer. It is the first program loaded when the computer is turned on, and its main component, the kernel, resides in memory at all times. The operating system sets the standards for all application programs (such as the Web server) that run in the computer. The applications communicate with the operating system for most user interface and file management operations.

Patch—A "repair job" for a piece of programming; also known as a "fix." A patch is the immediate solution that is provided to users; it can sometimes be downloaded from the software maker's Web site. The patch is not necessarily the best solution for the problem, and product developers often find a better solution to provide when they package the product for its next release. A patch is usually developed and distributed as a replacement for or an insertion in compiled code (that is, in a binary file or object module). In many operating systems, a special program is provided to manage and track the installation of patches.

Pharming—Using technical means to redirect users into accessing a fake Web site masquerading as a legitimate one and divulging personal information.

Phishing—Using social engineering techniques to trick users into accessing a fake Web site and divulging personal information.

Proxy—A proxy is an application that "breaks" the connection between client and server. The proxy accepts certain types of traffic entering or leaving a network, processes it, and forwards it. This effectively closes the straight path between the internal and external networks, making it more difficult for an attacker to obtain internal addresses and other details of the organization's internal network. Proxy servers are available for common Internet services; for example, a Hypertext Transfer Protocol (HTTP) proxy used for Web access and a Simple Mail Transfer Protocol (SMTP) proxy used for e-mail.

Service Pack—Microsoft's term for a collection of patches integrated into a single large update.

SOCKS Protocol—An Internet protocol to allow client applications to form a circuit-level gateway to a network firewall via a proxy service.

System Administrator—A person who manages a computer system, including its operating system and applications. A system administrator's responsibilities are similar to that of a network administrator.

Virtualization—The use of an abstraction layer to simulate computing hardware so that multiple operating systems can run on a single computer.

Vulnerability—A security exposure in an operating system or other system software or application software component. A variety of organizations maintain publicly accessible databases of vulnerabilities based on the version numbers of software. Each vulnerability can potentially compromise the system or network if exploited.

Web Server—A computer that provides World Wide Web (WWW) services on the Internet. It includes the hardware, operating system, Web server software, and Web site content (Web pages). If the Web server is used internally and not by the public, it may be known as an "intranet server."

Web Server Administrator—The Web server equivalent of a system administrator. Web server administrators are system architects responsible for the overall design, implementation, and maintenance of Web servers. They may or may not be responsible for Web content, which is traditionally the responsibility of the Webmaster.

Webmaster—A person responsible for the implementation of a Web site. Webmasters must be proficient in HTML and one or more scripting and interface languages, such as JavaScript and Perl. They may or may not be responsible for the underlying server, which is traditionally the responsibility of the Web administrator (see above).

Appendix C—Web Security Tools and Applications

The tools and applications referenced in this appendix are by no means a complete list of tools and applications to use for Web security, nor does this publication imply any endorsement of certain products.

Log File Analysis Tools

Tool	Capability	Web Site	Linux/ Unix	Win32	Cost
Analog	Most common OSs	http://www.analog.cx/intro.html	✓	✓	Free
Description	Analog is an automated Web server log file analysis tool that will compile on nearly any platform that supports the C programming language.				
Cronolog	Linux/Unix	http://www.cronolog.org/	✓		Free
Description	Cronolog is a program that reads log messages from its input and writes them to a set of output files constructed using a template and the current date and time.				
LiveStats6	Most Web servers and OSs	http://www.deepmetrix.com/	✓	✓	$$$
Description	Livestat6 is an automated Web server log file analysis tool.				
NetTracker	Most Web servers and OSs	http://www.unica.com/	✓	✓	$$$
Description	NetTracker is an automated Web server log file analysis tool.				
Swatch	Linux/Unix	http://swatch.sourceforge.net/	✓		Free
Description	Swatch is a Linux/Unix syslog analysis utility.				
Wwwstat	Linux and Unix with Perl installed	http://ftp.ics.uci.edu/pub/websoft/wwwstat/	✓		Free
Description	Wwwstat is an automated Web server log file analysis tool for common log file format access_log files.				

$$$=This product involves a fee.

Vulnerability Scanning Tools

Tool	Capability	Web Site	Linux/ Unix	Win32	Cost
Internet Security Systems (ISS) Internet Scanner	Vulnerability scanner	http://www.iss.net/		✓	$$$
Description	ISS Internet Scanner is a network-based vulnerability-scanning tool that identifies security holes on network hosts.				
Metasploit	Vulnerability scanner	http://www.metasploit.com/	✓	✓	Free
Description	Metasploit is a freeware vulnerability-scanning tool that identifies security holes on network hosts.				
Nessus	Vulnerability scanner	http://www.nessus.org/	✓	✓	Free

Tool	Capability	Web Site	Linux/ Unix	Win32	Cost
Description	*Nessus is a freeware network-based vulnerability-scanning tool that identifies security holes on network hosts.*				
Retina	Vulnerability scanner	http://www.eeye.com/		✓	$$$
Description	*Retina is a general-purpose network security scanner that identifies a large number of Web server vulnerabilities.*				
SAINT	Vulnerability scanner	http://www.saintcorporation.com/	✓		$$$
Description	*SAINT is a network-based vulnerability-scanning tool that identifies security holes on network hosts.*				
SARA	Vulnerability scanner	http://www-arc.com/sara/	✓		Free
Description	*SARA is a freeware network-based vulnerability-scanning tool that identifies security holes on network hosts.*				

$$$=This product involves a fee.

Web Application Scanning Tools

Tool	Capability	Web Site	Linux/ Unix	Win32	Cost
Acunetix	Web vulnerability scanner	http://www.acunetix.com/	✓		$$$
Description	*Acunetix Web vulnerability scanner is a Web application vulnerability scanner.*				
AppScan	Web vulnerability scanner	http://www.watchfire.com/		✓	$$$
Description	*AppScan is a Web application vulnerability scanner.*				
Nikto	Common Gateway Interface (CGI) vulnerability scanner	http://www.cirt.net/code/nikto.shtml	✓	✓	Free
Description	*Nikto is scanner that identifies vulnerabilities in CGI scripts.*				
Paros	Web proxy for security testing Web applications	http://www.parosproxy.org/index.shtml	✓	✓	Free
Description	*Paros allows for the interception and modification of all Hypertext Transfer Protocol (HTTP) and Secure Hypertext Transfer Protocol (HTTPS) data between server and client, including cookies and form fields, and allows for the testing of Web application security.*				
SiteDigger	A Web vulnerability scanner that looks at Google's data on your site	http://www.foundstone.com/us/resources/proddesc/sitedigger.htm		✓	Free
Description	*SiteDigger searches Google's cache to look for vulnerabilities, errors, configuration issues, proprietary information, and interesting security nuggets on Web sites.*				
SSLDigger	SSL cipher interrogator	http://www.foundstone.com/us/resources/proddesc/ssldigger.htm		✓	Free

Tool	Capability	Web Site	Linux/ Unix	Win32	Cost
Description	SSLDigger is a tool used to assess the strength of SSL servers by testing the ciphers supported. Some of these ciphers are known to be insecure.				
Wapiti	Web vulnerability scanner	http://wapiti.sourceforge.net/	✓	✓	Free
Description	*Wapiti is an open-source Web application vulnerability scanner.*				
WebInspect	Web vulnerability scanner	http://www.spidynamics.com/	✓	✓	$$$
Description	*WebInspect is a Web application vulnerability scanner.*				
WebScarab	Web application assessment tool	http://www.owasp.org/index.php/Category: OWASP_WebScarab_Project		✓	Free
Description	*WebScarab is a framework for analyzing applications that communicate using the HTTP and HTTPS protocols.*				
Wikto	Web server assessment tool	http://www.sensepost.com/research/wikto/		✓	Free
Description	*Wikto is a Web server and Web application vulnerability scanner.*				

$$$=This product involves a fee.

Appendix D—References

[Alle00]   Julia Allen et al., *Securing Network Servers*, April 2000,
               http://www.sei.cmu.edu/pub/documents/sims/pdf/sim010.pdf

[APWG07]   Anti-Phishing Working Group, *Vendor Solutions*, February 2007,
               http://www.antiphishing.org/solutions.html

[Bell06]   Steve Bellovin, "Unconventional Wisdom," *IEEE Security & Privacy*, Vol. 4, Issue 1,
               Jan–Feb 2006, page 88

[Chow02]   Pete Chown, *Advanced Encryption Standard (AES) Ciphersuites for Transport Layer
               Security (TLS)*, RFC 3268, January 2002, http://www.ietf.org/rfc/rfc3268.txt

[Coop01]   Russ Cooper, *10 Steps to Better IIS Security*, Information Security Magazine, August
               2001, http://www.infosecuritymag.com/articles/september01/features_IIS_security.shtml

[Curt01]   Matt Curtin, *Developing Trust: Online Privacy and Security*, November 2001

[FTC02]   Federal Trade Commission, *Email Address Harvesting: How Spammers Reap What You
               Sow*, November 2002, http://www.onguardonline.gov/spam.html

[FTC06]   Federal Trade Commission, *Pretexting: Your Personal Information Revealed*, February
               2006, http://www.ftc.gov/bcp/conline/pubs/credit/pretext.htm

[FTC06a]   Federal Trade Commission, *How Not to Get Hooked by a 'Phishing' Scam*, October
               2006, http://www.ftc.gov/bcp/edu/pubs/consumer/alerts/alt127.htm

[Google05]   Google, *Preventing Comment Spam*, January 2005,
               http://googleblog.blogspot.com/2005/01/preventing-comment-spam.html

[Johanson05]   Eric Johanson, *The state of homograph attacks*, February 2005,
               http://www.shmoo.com/idn/homograph.txt

[Koss00]   Klaus-Peter Kossakowski and Julia Allen, *Securing Public Web Servers*, 2000,
               http://www.sei.cmu.edu/pub/documents/sims/pdf/sim011.pdf

[MASS99]   Commonwealth of Massachusetts, Executive Order 412, 1999,
               http://www.state.ma.us/consumer/New/privexeco.htm

[Netcraft06]   Netcraft, *PayPal Security Flaw Allows Identity Theft*, June 2006,
               http://news.netcraft.com/archives/2006/06/16/paypal_security_flaw_allows_identity_thef
               t.html

[NISS99]   National Information System Security Glossary, NSTISSI No. 4009, January 1999

[NIST01]   Wayne A. Jansen, NIST Special Publication 800-28, *Guidelines on Active Content and
               Mobile Code*, October 2001, http://csrc.nist.gov/publications/nistpubs/index.html

[NIST02a]   John Wack et al., NIST Special Publication 800-41, *Guidelines on Firewalls and
               Firewall Policy*, January 2002, http://csrc.nist.gov/publications/nistpubs/index.html

[NIST02b]   John Wack et al., NIST Special Publication 800-42, *Guideline on Network Security Testing*, February 2002, http://csrc.nist.gov/publications/nistpubs/index.html

[NIST06a]   Marianne Swanson et al., NIST Special Publication 800-18 Revision 1, *Guide for Developing Security Plans for Federal Information Systems*, February 2006, http://csrc.nist.gov/publications/nistpubs/index.html

[NIST06b]   Karen Kent and Murugiah Souppaya, NIST Special Publication 800-92, *Guide to Computer Security Log Management*, April 2006, http://csrc.nist.gov/publications/nistpubs/index.html

[NIST06c]   Miles Tracy et al., NIST Special Publication 800-45, Version 2, *Guidelines on Electronic Mail Security*, February 2007, http://csrc.nist.gov/publications/nistpubs/index.html

[NIST07]   Karen Scarfone and Peter Mell, NIST Special Publication 800-94, *Guide to Intrusion Detection and Prevention Systems (IDPS)*, February 2007, http://csrc.nist.gov/publications/nistpubs/index.html

[NVD06]   National Vulnerability Database, *CVE-2005-0233*, September 2006, http://nvd.nist.gov/nvd.cfm?cvename=CVE-2005-0233

[Ollm04]   Gunter Ollman, *The Phishing Guide: Understanding and Preventing Phishing Attacks*, NGSSoftware, September 2004, http://www.nextgenss.com/papers/NISR-WP-Phishing.pdf

[Ollm05]   Gunter Ollman, *The Pharming Guide: Understanding and Preventing DNS-Related Attacks by Phishers*, NGSSoftware, August 2005, http://www.nextgenss.com/papers/ThePharmingGuide.pdf

[OMB00a]   Office of Management and Budget Memorandum 2000-13, 2000, http://www.whitehouse.gov/omb/memoranda/m00-13.html

[OMB00b]   Office of Management and Budget Cookie Clarification Letter 1, 2000, http://www.whitehouse.gov/omb/inforeg/cookies_letter72800.html

[OMB00c]   Office of Management and Budget Cookie Clarification Letter 2, 2000, http://www.whitehouse.gov/omb/inforeg/cookies_letter90500.html

[OWASP06]   Open Web Application Security Project (OWASP), *OWASP Guide*, March 2006, http://owasp.cvs.sourceforge.net/*checkout*/owasp/guide/current%20draft.pdf

[RSA00]   *PKCS #10 Version 1.7, Certification Request Syntax Standard*, May 26, 2000, ftp://ftp.rsasecurity.com/pub/pkcs/pkcs-10/pkcs-10v1_7.pdf

[Salt75]   Jerome H. Saltzer and Michael Schroeder, "The Protection of Information in Computer Systems," *Proceedings of the IEEE*, Vol. 63, pages 1278–1308

[Scam01]   Joel Scambray et al., *Hacking Exposed Second Edition*, McGraw-Hill, 2001

[Schn00]   Bruce Schneier, *Secrets & Lies: Digital Security in a Networked World*, John Wiley & Sons Inc., 2000

[SPID06]   SPI Dynamics, *AJAX Security Dangers*, 2006,
            http://www.spidynamics.com/assets/documents/AJAXdangers.pdf

[SSL98]   *Introduction to SSL, Netscape Communication*, Netscape Corporation, 1998,
            http://docs.sun.com/source/816-6156-10/contents.htm

[Unsp06]   Unspam Technologies, *How to Avoid Being Harvested by Spambots*,
            http://www.projecthoneypot.org/how_to_avoid_spambots.php

[Whit06]   James A. Whittaker, "How to Think About Security," *IEEE Security & Privacy*, Vol. 4,
            Issue 2, Mar–Apr 2006, pages 68–71

[WWW01]   *The World Wide Web Security FAQ*, September 2001, http://www.w3.org/Security/Faq/

[Ziri02]   Neal Ziring, *Web Server Execution: System and Security Issues*, presented to Information
            Assurance Technical Framework Forum, March 1, 2002

Appendix E—Web Server Security Checklist

This section provides a combined version of the individual security checklists provided at the end of many sections in this document.

Planning and Managing Web Servers

Completed	Action
	Plan the configuration and deployment of the Web server
☐	Identify functions of the Web server
☐	Identify categories of information that will be stored, processed, and transmitted through the Web server
☐	Identify security requirements of information
☐	Identify how information is published to the Web server
☐	Identify the security requirements of other hosts involved (e.g., backend database or Web service)
☐	Identify a dedicated host to run the Web server
☐	Identify network services that will be provided or supported by the Web server
☐	Identify the security requirements of any additional services provided or supported by the Web server
☐	Identify how the Web server will be managed
☐	Identify users and categories of users of the Web server and determine privilege for each category of user
☐	Identify user authentication methods for the Web server and how authentication data will be protected
☐	Identify how access to information resources will be enforced
☐	Identify appropriate physical security mechanisms
☐	Identify appropriate availability mechanisms
	Choose appropriate OS for Web server
☐	Minimal exposure to vulnerabilities
☐	Ability to restrict administrative or root level activities to authorized users only
☐	Ability to control access to data on the server
☐	Ability to disable unnecessary network services that may be built into the OS or server software
☐	Ability to control access to various forms of executable programs, such as CGI scripts and server plug-ins
☐	Ability to log appropriate server activities to detect intrusions and attempted intrusions
☐	Provision of a host-based firewall capability
☐	Availability of experienced staff to install, configure, secure, and maintain OS
	Choose appropriate platform for Web server
☐	General purpose OS Trusted OS Web server appliance Pre-hardened OS and Web server Virtualized platform

Securing the Web Server Operating System

Completed	Action
	Patch and upgrade OS
☐	Create, document, and implement a patching process
☐	Keep the servers disconnected from networks or on an isolated network that severely restricts communications until all patches have been installed
☐	Identify and install all necessary patches and upgrades to the OS
☐	Identify and install all necessary patches and upgrades to applications and services included with the OS
☐	Identify and mitigate any unpatched vulnerabilities
	Remove or disable unnecessary services and applications
☐	Disable or remove unnecessary services and applications
	Configure OS user authentication
☐	Remove or disable unneeded default accounts and groups
☐	Disable non-interactive accounts
☐	Create the user groups for the particular computer
☐	Create the user accounts for the particular computer
☐	Check the organization's password policy and set account passwords appropriately (e.g., length, complexity)
☐	Prevent password guessing (e.g., increase the period between attempts, deny login after a defined number of failed attempts)
☐	Install and configure other security mechanisms to strengthen authentication
	Configure resource controls appropriately
☐	Deny read access to unnecessary files and directories
☐	Deny write access to unnecessary files and directories
☐	Limit the execution privilege of system tools to system administrators
	Install and configure additional security controls
☐	Select, install, and configure additional software to provide needed controls not included in the OS, such as antivirus software, antispyware software, rootkit detectors, host-based intrusion detection and prevention software, host-based firewalls, and patch management software
	Test the security of the OS
☐	Identify a separate identical system
☐	Test OS after initial install to determine vulnerabilities
☐	Test OS periodically (e.g., quarterly) to determine new vulnerabilities

Securing the Web Server

Completed	Action
	Securely install the Web server
☐	Install the Web server software on a dedicated host or a dedicated virtualized guest OS
☐	Apply any patches or upgrades to correct for known vulnerabilities
☐	Create a dedicated physical disk or logical partition (separate from OS and Web server application) for Web content

Completed	Action
☐	Remove or disable all services installed by the Web server application but not required (e.g., gopher, FTP, remote administration)
☐	Remove or disable all unneeded default login accounts created by the Web server installation
☐	Remove all manufacturer documentation from server
☐	Remove any example or test files from server, including scripts and executable code
☐	Apply appropriate security template or hardening script to the server
☐	Reconfigure HTTP service banner (and others as required) NOT to report Web server and OS type and version
	Configure OS and Web server access controls
☐	Configure the Web server process to run as a user with a strictly limited set of privileges
☐	Configure the Web server so that Web content files can be read but not written by service processes
☐	Configure the Web server so that service processes cannot write to the directories where public Web content is stored
☐	Configure the Web server so that only processes authorized for Web server administration can write Web content files
☐	Configure the host OS so that the Web server can write log files but not read them
☐	Configure the host OS so that temporary files created by the Web server application are restricted to a specified and appropriately protected subdirectory
☐	Configure the host OS so that access to any temporary files created by the Web server application is limited to the service processes that created the files
☐	Install Web content on a different hard drive or logical partition than the OS and Web server application
☐	If uploads are allowed to the Web server, configure it so that a limit is placed on the amount of hard drive space that is dedicated for this purpose; uploads should be placed on a separate partition
☐	Ensure that log files are stored in a location that is sized appropriately; log files should be placed on a separate partition
☐	Configure the maximum number of Web server processes and/or network connections that the Web server should allow
☐	Ensure that any virtualized guest OSs follow this checklist
☐	Ensure users and administrators are able to change passwords
☐	Disable users after a specified period of inactivity
☐	Ensure each user and administrator has a unique ID
	Configure a secure Web content directory
☐	Dedicate a single hard drive or logical partition for Web content and establish related subdirectories exclusively for Web server content files, including graphics but excluding scripts and other programs
☐	Define a single directory exclusively for all external scripts or programs executed as part of Web server content (e.g., CGI, ASP)
☐	Disable the execution of scripts that are not exclusively under the control of administrative accounts. This action is accomplished by creating and controlling access to a separate directory intended to contain authorized scripts
☐	Disable the use of hard or symbolic links (e.g., shortcuts for Windows)

Completed	Action
☐	Define a complete Web content access matrix. Identify which folders and files within the Web server document should be restricted and which should be accessible (and by whom)
☐	Check the organization's password policy and set account passwords appropriately (e.g., length, complexity)
☐	Use the robots.txt file, if appropriate
☐	Configure anti-spambot protection, if appropriate (e.g., CAPTCHAs, nofollow, or keyword filtering)

Securing Web Content

Completed	Action
	Ensure that none of the following types of information are available on or through a public Web server
☐	Classified records
☐	Internal personnel rules and procedures
☐	Sensitive or proprietary information
☐	Personal information about an organization's personnel
☐	Telephone numbers, e-mail addresses, or general listings of staff unless necessary to fulfill organizational requirements
☐	Schedules of organizational principals or their exact location (whether on or off the premises)
☐	Information on the composition, preparation, or optimal use of hazardous materials or toxins
☐	Sensitive information relating to homeland security
☐	Investigative records
☐	Financial records (beyond those already publicly available)
☐	Medical records
☐	Organization's physical and information security procedures
☐	Information about organization's network and information system infrastructure
☐	Information that specifies or implies physical security vulnerabilities
☐	Plans, maps, diagrams, aerial photographs, and architectural plans of organizational building, properties, or installations
☐	Copyrighted material without the written permission of the owner
☐	Privacy or security policies that indicate the types of security measures in place to the degree that they may be useful to an attacker
	Establish an organizational-wide documented formal policy and process for approving public Web content that—
☐	Identifies information that should be published on the Web
☐	Identifies target audience
☐	Identifies possible negative ramifications of publishing the information
☐	Identifies who should be responsible for creating, publishing, and maintaining this particular information
☐	Provides guidelines on styles and formats appropriate for Web publishing
☐	Provides for appropriate review of the information for sensitivity and distribution/release controls (including the sensitivity of the information in aggregate)

Completed	Action
☐	Determines the appropriate access and security controls
☐	Provides guidance on the information contained within the source code of the Web content
	Maintain Web user privacy
☐	Maintain a published privacy policy
☐	Prohibit the collection of personally identifying data without the explicit permission of the user and collect only the data that is absolutely needed
☐	Prohibit the use of "persistent" cookies
☐	Use the session cookie only if it is clearly identified in published privacy policy
	Mitigate indirect attacks on content
☐	Ensure users of the site are aware of the dangers of phishing and pharming attacks and how to avoid them
☐	Validate official communication by personalizing emails and providing unique identifying (but not confidential) information only the organization and user should know
☐	Use digital signatures on e-mail if appropriate
☐	Perform content validation within the Web application to prevent more sophisticated phishing attacks (e.g., cross-site scripting based attacks)
☐	Personalize Web content to aid in users' identifying fraudulent Web sites
☐	Use token-based or mutual authentication if applicable
☐	Suggest the use of Web browsers or browser toolbars with phishing/ pharming protection
☐	Use current versions of DNS software with the latest security patches
☐	Install server-side DNS protection mechanisms
☐	Monitor organizational domains and similar domains
☐	Simplify the structure of organization domain names
☐	Use secure connections for logins
☐	If necessary, engage a vendor to provide stronger anti-phishing/ anti-pharming measures
	Client-side active content security considerations
☐	Weigh the risks and benefits of client-side active content
☐	Take no actions without the express permission of user
☐	When possible, only use widely-adopted active content such as JavaScript, PDF, and Flash
☐	When possible, provide alternatives (e.g., HTML provided along with PDF)
	Maintain server-side active content security
☐	Only simple, easy-to-understand code should be used
☐	Limited or no reading or writing to the file system should be permitted
☐	Limited or no interaction with other programs (e.g., sendmail) should be permitted
☐	There should be no requirement to run with suid privileges on Unix or Linux
☐	Explicit path names should be used (i.e., does not rely on path variable)
☐	No directories have both write and execute permissions
☐	All executable files are placed in a dedicated folders
☐	SSIs are disabled or the execute function is disabled
☐	All user input is validated

Completed	Action
☐	Web content generation code should be scanned or audited
☐	Dynamically created pages do not create dangerous metacharacters
☐	Character set encoding should be explicitly set in each page
☐	User data should be scanned to ensure it contains only expected input, (e.g., a-z, A-Z, 0-9); care should be taken with special characters or HTML tags
☐	Cookies should be examined for any special characters
☐	Encryption mechanism is used to encrypt passwords entered through scripts forms
☐	For Web applications that are restricted by username and password, none of the Web pages in the application should be accessible without executing the appropriate login process
☐	All sample scripts are removed
☐	No third-party scripts or executable code are used without verifying the source code

Using Authentication and Encryption Technologies for Web Servers

Completed	Action
	Configure Web authentication and encryption technologies
☐	For Web resources that require minimal protection and for which there is a small, clearly defined audience, configure address-based authentication
☐	For Web resources that require additional protection but for which there is a small, clearly defined audience, configure address-based authentication as a second line of defense
☐	For Web resources that require minimal protection but for which there is no clearly defined audience, configure basic or digest authentication (better)
☐	For Web resources that require protection from malicious bots, configure basic or digest authentication (better) or implement mitigation techniques discussed in Section 5.2.4
☐	For organizations required to comply with FIPS 140-2, ensure the SSL/TLS implementation is FIPS-validated
☐	For Web resources that require maximum protection, configure SSL/TLS
	Configure SSL/TLS
☐	Ensure the SSL/TLS implementation is fully patched
☐	Use a third-party issued certificate for server authentication (unless all systems using the server are organization-managed, in which case a self-signed certificate could potentially be used instead)
☐	For configurations that require a medium level of client authentication, configure server to require username and password via SSL/TLS
☐	For configurations that require a high level of client authentication, configure server to require client certificates via SSL/TLS
☐	Ensure weak cipher suites are disabled (see Table 7.1 for the recommended usage of Federal cipher suites)
☐	Configure file integrity checker to monitor Web server certificate
☐	If only SSL/TLS is to be used in the Web server, ensure access via any TCP port other than 443 is disabled
☐	If most traffic to the Web server will be via encrypted SSL/TLS, ensure that appropriate logging and detection mechanisms are employed in the Web server (because network monitoring is ineffective against encrypted SSL/TLS sessions)

Completed	Action
	Protect against brute force attacks
☐	Use strong authentication if possible
☐	Use a delay after failed login attempts
☐	Lock out an account after a set number of failed login attempts
☐	Enforce a password policy
☐	Blacklist IP addresses or domains known to attempt brute force attacks
☐	Use log monitoring software to detect brute force attacks

Implementing a Secure Network Infrastructure

Completed	Action
	Identify network location
☐	Web server is located in a DMZ, or Web server hosting is outsourced
	Assess firewall configuration
☐	Web server is protected by a firewall; if it faces a higher threat or is more vulnerable, it is protected by an application layer firewall
☐	Firewall controls all traffic between the Internet and the Web server
☐	Firewall blocks all inbound traffic to the Web server except TCP ports 80 (HTTP) and/or 443 (HTTPS), if required
☐	Firewall blocks (in conjunction with the IDPS) IP addresses or subnets that the IDPS reports are attacking the organizational network
☐	Firewall notifies the network or Web server administrator of suspicious activity through an appropriate means
☐	Firewall provides content filtering (application layer firewall)
☐	Firewall is configured to protect against DoS attacks
☐	Firewall detects malformed or known attack URL requests
☐	Firewall logs critical events
☐	Firewall and firewall OS are patched to latest or most secure level
	Evaluate intrusion detection and prevention systems
☐	Host-based IDPS is used for Web servers that operate primarily using SSL/TLS
☐	IDPS is configured to monitor network traffic to and from the Web server after firewall
☐	IDPS is configured to monitor changes to critical files on Web server (host-based IDPS or file integrity checker)
☐	IDPS blocks (in conjunction with the firewall) IP addresses or subnets that are attacking the organizational network
☐	IDPS notifies the IDPS administrators or Web server administrator of attacks through appropriate means
☐	IDPS is configured to maximize detection with an acceptable level of false positives
☐	IDPS is configured to log events
☐	IDPS is updated with new attack signatures frequently (e.g., on a daily basis)
☐	Host-based IDPS is configured to monitor the system resources available in the Web server host
	Assess network switches
☐	Switches are used to protect against network eavesdropping

Completed	Action
☐	Switches are configured in high-security mode to defeat ARP spoofing and ARP poisoning attacks
☐	Switches are configured to send all traffic on network segment to network-based IDPS
	Evaluate load balancers
☐	Load balancers are used to increase Web server availability
☐	Load balancers are augmented by Web caches if applicable
	Evaluate reverse proxies
☐	Reverse proxies are used as a security gateway to increase Web server availability
☐	Reverse proxies are augmented with encryption acceleration, user authentication, and content filtering capabilities, if applicable

Administering the Web Server

Completed	Action
	Perform logging
☐	Use the combined log format for storing the Transfer Log or manually configure the information described by the combined log format to be the standard format for the Transfer Log
☐	Enable the Referrer Log or Agent Log if the combined log format is unavailable
☐	Establish different log file names for different virtual Web sites that may be implemented as part of a single physical Web server
☐	Use the remote user identity as specified in RFC 1413
☐	Store logs on a separate (syslog) host
☐	Ensure there is sufficient capacity for the logs
☐	Archive logs according to organizational requirements
☐	Review logs daily
☐	Review logs weekly (for more long-term trends)
☐	Use automated log file analysis tool(s)
	Perform Web server backups
☐	Create a Web server backup policy
☐	Back up Web server differentially or incrementally on a daily to weekly basis
☐	Back up Web server fully on a weekly to monthly basis
☐	Periodically archive backups
☐	Maintain an authoritative copy of Web site(s)
	Recover from a compromise
☐	Report the incident to the organization's computer incident response capability
☐	Isolate the compromised system(s) or take other steps to contain the attack so additional information can be collected
☐	Investigate similar hosts to determine if the attacker has also compromised other systems
☐	Consult, as appropriate, with management, legal counsel, and law enforcement officials expeditiously
☐	Analyze the intrusion
☐	Restore the system

Completed	Action
☐	Test system to ensure security
☐	Reconnect system to network
☐	Monitor system and network for signs that the attacker is attempting to access the system or network again
☐	Document lessons learned
	Test security
☐	Periodically conduct vulnerability scans on Web server, dynamically generated content, and supporting network
☐	Update vulnerability scanner prior to testing
☐	Correct any deficiencies identified by the vulnerability scanner
☐	Conduct penetration testing on the Web server and the supporting network infrastructure
☐	Correct deficiencies identified by penetration testing
	Conduct remote administration and content updates
☐	Use a strong authentication mechanism (e.g., public/private key pair, two-factor authentication)
☐	Restrict hosts that can be used to remotely administer or update content on the Web server by IP address and to the internal network
☐	Use secure protocols (e.g., SSH, HTTPS)
☐	Enforce the concept of least privilege on remote administration and content updating (e.g., attempt to minimize the access rights for the remote administration/update accounts)
☐	Change any default accounts or passwords from the remote administration utility or application
☐	Do not allow remote administration from the Internet unless mechanisms such as VPNs are used
☐	Do not mount any file shares on the internal network from the Web server or vice versa

Appendix F—Acronym List

3DES	Triple Data Encryption Standard
ACL	Access Control List
ADA	American Disability Association
AES	Advanced Encryption Standard
AIRWeb	Adversarial Information Retrieval on the Web
AJAX	Asynchronous JavaScript and XML
API	Application Programming Interface
APWG	Anti-Phishing Working Group
ARP	Address Resolution Protocol
ASCII	American Standard Code of Information Interchange
ASP	Active Server Page
CA	Certificate Authority
CAPTCHA	Completely Automated Public Turing Test to Tell Computers and Humans Apart
CD-R	Compact Disc Recordable
CERIAS	Center for Education and Research in Information Assurance and Security
CERT/CC	Computer Emergency Response Team Coordination Center
CIAC	Computer Incident Advisory Capability (U.S. Department of Energy)
CIO	Chief Information Officer
CGI	Common Gateway Interface
CLF	Common Log Format
CMVP	Cryptographic Module Validation Program
CN	Common Name
CPU	Central Processing Unit
CSR	Certificate-Signing Request
DDoS	Distributed Denial of Service
DES	Data Encryption Standard
DHS	Department of Homeland Security
DMZ	Demilitarized Zone
DN	Domain Name
DNS	Domain Name System
DoD	Department of Defense
DoS	Denial of Service
DSS	Digital Signature Standard
FIPS	Federal Information Processing Standard
FISMA	Federal Information Security Management Act
FOIA	Freedom of Information Act
FTC	Federal Trade Commission
FTP	File Transfer Protocol
GUI	Graphical User Interface
HTCP	Hypertext Caching Protocol
HTML	Hypertext Markup Language
HTTP	Hypertext Transfer Protocol
HTTPS	Hypertext Transfer Protocol Secure

IBMJSSE	IBM Java Secure Sockets Extension
ICCC	Internet Crime Complaint Center
ICP	Internet Caching Protocol
IDPS	Intrusion Detection and Prevention System
IDS	Intrusion Detection System
IETF	Internet Engineering Task Force
IIS	Internet Information Server
IMAP	Internet Message Access Protocol
IP	Internet Protocol
IPS	Intrusion Prevention System
IPSec	Internet Protocol Security
IS	Information System
ISP	Internet Service Provider
ISS	Internet Security Systems
ISSO	Information System Security Officer
ISSPM	Information Systems Security Program Manager
IT	Information Technology
ITL	Information Technology Laboratory
JRE	Java Runtime Environment
JSSE	Java Secure Socket Extension
JSP	Java Server Page
JVM	Java Virtual Machine
LAN	Local Area Network
LDAP	Lightweight Directory Access Protocol
MAC	Message Authentication Code
NARA	National Archives and Records Administration
NetBIOS	Network Basic Input/Output System
NFS	Network File System
NIS	Network Information System
NIST	National Institute of Standards and Technology
NSA	National Security Agency
NSS	Network Security Services
NVD	National Vulnerability Database
ODBC	Open Database Connectivity
OMB	Office of Management and Budget
OS	Operating System
OWASP	Open Web Application Security Project
PC	Personal Computer
PDF	Portable Document Format
PEM	Privacy Enhanced Mail
PHP	PHP Hypertext Preprocessor
PII	Personally Identifiable Information
PKCS	Public Key Cryptography Standard
PKI	Public Key Infrastructure

RAID	Redundant Array of Inexpensive Disks
REP	Robots Exclusion Protocol
RFC	Request for Comments
SHA-1	Secure Hash Algorithm-1
SHS	Secure Hash Standard
SIEM	Security Information and Event Management
SMTP	Simple Mail Transfer Protocol
SNMP	Simple Network Management Protocol
SOHO	Small Office Home Office
SP	Special Publication
SQL	Structured Query Language
SSH	Secure Shell
SSI	Server Side Includes
SSL	Secure Sockets Layer
SSN	Social Security Number
SSPI	Security Support Provider Interface
TCP	Transmission Control Protocol
TLS	Transport Layer Security
TOS	Trusted Operating System
UDP	User Datagram Protocol
UMBC	University of Maryland Baltimore County
URI	Uniform Resource Identifier
URL	Uniform Resource Locator
U.S.	United States
US-CERT	United States Computer Emergency Response Team
VLAN	Virtual Local Area Network
VPN	Virtual Private Network
WCCP	Web Cache Coordination Protocol
WWW	World Wide Web
XML	Extensible Markup Language
XSS	Cross-Site Scripting